Elias

An Epic of the Ages

Orson F. Whitney

Alpha Editions

This edition published in 2021

ISBN : 9789354595479

Design and Setting By
Alpha Editions
www.alphaedis.com
Email - info@alphaedis.com

As per information held with us this book is in Public Domain. This book is a reproduction of an important historical work. Alpha Editions uses the best technology to reproduce historical work in the same manner it was first published to preserve its original nature. Any marks or number seen are left intentionally to preserve its true form.

Contents

FOREWORD	- 1 -
DEDICATION	- 2 -
THEME	- 3 -
ARGUMENT	- 4 -
PRELUDE	- 5 -
CANTO ONE	- 6 -
CANTO TWO	- 12 -
CANTO THREE	- 18 -
CANTO FOUR	- 25 -
CANTO FIVE	- 34 -
CANTO SIX	- 44 -
CANTO SEVEN	- 59 -
CANTO EIGHT	- 69 -
CANTO NINE	- 79 -
CANTO TEN	- 86 -
EPILOGUE	- 94 -
NOTES	- 98 -

FOREWORD

"Elias" was begun in the spring of 1900, and was first published in the autumn of 1904, when an edition de luxe, limited to one hundred and fifty copies, and two less pretentious editions, were subscribed for by friends of the author. He was hardly a party to the project, the initial step being taken without his knowledge. Prior to that time he had read the poem to select gatherings in private homes and in two of the leading church schools, but had no thought of printing it so early, until solicited by a committee of prominent citizens to allow them to undertake, in his behalf, its publication.

That committee consisted of Governor Heber M. Wells, Senator George Sutherland, President Anthon H. Lund, Major Richard W. Young, and Mr. H. L. A. Culmer. These gentlemen, out of pure public spirit and a friendly feeling for the author, had associated themselves together for this purpose. Though aware of many defects in his work, and anxious to mend them before facing the public and the critics, he nevertheless accepted gratefully the very generous offer. All the members of the committee gave to the enterprise their hearty support, and two of them, Major Young and Mr. Culmer, conducted most of the business necessary to putting the book through the press.

Since the original issuance the author has endeavored to bring the work into a more finished state, and the results are now before the reader. The poem is in twelve parts—a prelude, ten cantos, and an epilogue. Following these are explanatory notes, for the benefit of students; the introduction of the epic as a text book into the schools being one of the purposes for which it was written.

The character and scope of the work are partly indicated by the title, "Elias—An Epic Of The Ages." It is an attempt to present, in verse form, historically, doctrinally, and prophetically, the vast theme comprehended in what the world terms "Mormonism."

THE AUTHOR.

DEDICATION

(SEE NOTE.)

This song to thee, friend, chieftain, sixth to rise
From him, the foremost of a seeric line,
Mock of the worldly, marvel of the wise,—
His martyred brother's son! May light divine,
Which 'lumined them, forever on thee shine,
Flooding with splendors new thy lineal fame;
And ancient rays with modern beams combine
To glorify a brow whose stalwart aim,
To merit heaven's high praise, nor fear a world's false blame!

THEME

(SEE NOTE.)

"And if you will receive it, this is Elias, which was to come to gather together the tribes of Israel and restore all things."

ARGUMENT

The aim of this poem is to point out those manifestations of the Divine Mind and those impulsions from human enterprise which have contributed in all ages to the progress of the race toward perfection.

Thus it deals not only with man's origin and destiny, with earth's creation, redemption, and ultimate glorification, but with events and epochs leading up to and having those greater ends as their decreed consummation. The Christ theme, in its heavenly and earthly phases, is supplemented by the sacred and secular history of man upon both hemispheres. God's direct dealings through prophets, apostles, and other inspired agents, and His indirect dealings through poets, painters, philosophers, inventors, discoverers, statesmen, kings, conquerors and the like, are indicated, and the experiences of the Church of Christ in various dispensations portrayed.

The title "Elias," signifying restoration and preparation,—the lesser going before the greater with those objects in view,—is used to denote and personify the Genius of Progress, whose beneficent workings, under the guidance of the Infinite Spirit, through the aeons and the ages, behind the scenes and upon the stage of human action, are the warp and woof of the entire poem. The medial point is the Dispensation of the Fulness of Times, the era of restitution, when the House of God is to be set in order, and all things in Christ are to be gathered into one.

PRELUDE

(SEE NOTE.)

    The work for Him I asked and aimed to do,
  Ere death should claim my dust, my spirit free,—
  That, looking down from where the wise and true
  Inherit glory, gracious eyes might see
  A spark I kindled beaming endlessly,
  And lighting other wanderers to the goal
  Where blends the life that is with life to be;—
  Now done, or well or ill, the lettered scroll
Of what is writ on heart and mind I here unroll.

CANTO ONE

As From a Dream[1]

Youth's morn was breaking, when I dreamed a dream,
Splendid as springtime's weft of wonders rare;
Idyllic vision, beauteous, bright romance,
Glory of love and glamor of renown.
I dreamed that fame held all of happiness,
Save the sweet charm that lurked in woman's smile.

Wealth wooed I not, nor power—to wear the sign
And wave the symbol of authority;
To speak, and have hosts tremble; or to frown,
And find all pale and prostrate at my feet. 10
But oh! to sway, like swinging forest boughs
In summer breeze, men's yearning hearts and minds,—
Sway them in duty's name, in virtue's cause,
By tongue of thunder or by pen of flame,
Leaving some wise, sublime, benefic deed,
Some word or work of merit and of might,
To fix the fleeting gaze of centuries!

Glory and love—these were my guides divine,
The planet passions of my destiny,
The Baal and Astoreth[2] to whom I bowed, 20
At human shrines a worldly worshiper,
Adoring beauteous dust, my fellow clay,
And coveting an earthly immortality.

And at the feet of these dear deities,
Careless of great Jehovah's smile or frown,
In the fresh morning of my youth's fair might,
Slumbering I dreamed, till golden grew the dawn.

A strange and stern awakening—a sky,
Pearl, gold, and sapphire, clear and calm till then,
Cloud-curtained, grim, with anger audible, 30
Tortured and torn with swift-flung darts of fire;
Booming and crashing, bolt on bolt descends;
Earth, air, and heaven are wrapt in roaring flame.

And when the rifted storm has rolled away,
And stillness reascends her solemn throne,
Ruin looks forth from retrospection's tower,
And memory weeps where desolation reigns.

It was the end. Dispelled illusion's dream.
Youth's fond ideals, thunder-stricken, strewn,
Lay level with the dust. But light had come! 40
My soul had cast its fetters and was free.

I slept and dreamed no more; I was awake!
And saw and heard with other eyes and ears,
Which taught me things unseen, unheard, before;
Things new yet old—old as eternity,
Old e'en to time, though new and strange to me.

I talked with Truth on solemn mountain tops;
I soared with winged thought the sunlit dome;
Studied the midnight stars; and when anon
The hurrying, far-flung legions of the storm 50
In supermortal might went forth to war,
Would fain have charioted the charging plain,
Or spurred the tempest as a battle steed,
Grasping the volted lightnings as they flew,
And thundering through the mists on things below.

Rejoicing in my new-found strength, I gave
Glory to Him, the Source and Sire of all;
That God whom I had neither loved nor feared,
That God whom now I worshipt and adored.
Who girdled me with Light, truth's triple key[3], 60
Unlocking what hath been, what yet shall be,
Probing death's gloom, life's three-fold mystery,
Solving the secret—Whither, Whence and Why.

Oh, wondrous transformation! when with wand
Of wakening might, that all-uplifting power
Waved o'er the cross where hung fond hopes impaled,
Waved o'er the tomb where loved ambitions lay,
Touched the strewn fragments of my shattered dream,
Bidding the dead arise in bodies new,
Building, on ruined hope, faith's battlement, 70
Love's palace, peace-domed, pinnacled in light,
In glory greater than earth's grandest dream,
Than glittering fame's most splendid spectacle;
Ideal transcending ideality,
Ideal made real past all reality!

Whose earth-dimmed eye could see what then I saw?
Whose earth-dulled ear such harmonies could hear?

When the all-searching Spirit tore the veil
Of things that seem, and showed me things that are.

    Beauty, both good and evil—lamp to heaven 80
Or lure-light o'er the marshes of despair.
Beauty, divine—but not divinity;
Not parent—child of purity and truth;
Nor fount, nor stream, but bubble lost in air,
Nor tree, nor fruit—only a fragrant flower,
Flung from ambrosial gardens[4], here to grow
That life might be the less a wilderness.

    But lo! a loveliness that blooms for aye,
That, withering here, is there revivified,
A loveliness made lovelier evermore; 90
The beauty of the restful and the risen,
Of Paradise[5] and Glory's higher home.

    Pure as the mountain monarch's ice-crowned crest,
Pure as the snow-king's mantle, diamond-strewn,
Pure as the cascade's limpid crystalline,
Leaping from cliff to chasm, the breeze-flung flood
Blown into spirit spray of dazzling sheen;
So pure the love that warmed my boyish breast,
And lit the yearning of my youthful eye.

    But pure love, e'en the purest, may be blind. 100
Truth spake—then fell the blindness from Love's eyes[6],
Revealing life in hues of hopefulness;
Love's rainbow dream, that only time's vale spans
To human vision, widening now till lost
Beyond the pale peaks of eternity.

    Heaven's gold love is, though mixt with earth's alloy—
Dross, that betimes a needful part doth play
In nature's wise and true economy.

    Love dies not—'t is love's seeming that dissolves,
Low to its serpent level, native dust, 110
A grave unmemoried in lethean ground[7].
The while see heaven-born, heaven-aspiring love,
Immortal spirit of the universe,
Soaring past sun and stars to worlds unknown!
Heir to herself, a self-succeeding queen,
Still regnant on life's throne when life is o'er.

O thou, of beauty[8], loveliest form and phase!
Kindler and keeper of the quenchless flame!
Partner and peer of human majesty!
Sharing with him life's dual sovereignty, 120
Well canst thou wait for thrones and diadems.
Queen of the future, Eve of coming worlds,
Mother of spirits that shall people stars,
And hail thee empress of a universe!

No more I deemed of crowning consequence,
That mortal clay to mortal eye should shine;
That human mites should shout and sing in praise
Each of the other's midget mightiness—
A molecule, by atoms glorified!

Apple of ashes[9] to the longing lip! 130
Brine to the burning throat and thirsting soul!
Phantom, delusion, misty ghost of fame!
Voidest and vainest of all vanities!

"Be not beguiled!" A vibrant thunder note,
Pealing from clouds that canopied my life,
The warning, lightning-winged to purify,
Up-kindling all the summits of the soul.
"Be not beguiled; not what men think and say,
But what God sees and knows, is what avails.

"Who knoweth aught, unknowing of the all? 140
Unknowing all, who knoweth perfectly
'Twixt small and great, 'twixt failure and success,
'Twixt heights of glory and the gulfs of shame?
What cares eternity for time's decrees?
Defeat hath oft deserved the conqueror's crown;
Dishonor worn the wreath of victory.

"Greatness—is it to loom 'mid glittering show?
Goes power but hand in hand with prominence?
Largeness or littleness, or high or low,
Has but to breathe, and straightway he is known. 150
What speech conceals, the spirit manifests.

"Fame, place, and title find a fitting use,
And rightfully demand all reverence due.
But envy not the empty lot of him
Who, winning without merit, wins in vain.

"Greatness, true greatness, mightiness of mind,
And greater greatness, grandeur of the soul,
Tell but one tale—capacity, not place;
Capacity, whose sire, experience,
Whose ancestors, innate intelligence, 160
Original, inborn nobility,
As oft in hut as mansion have their home.

"'Tis not the crowning that creates the king.
Man's proper place where God hath need of him.

"Naught can be vain that leadeth unto light;
Struggle and stress, not plaudit, maketh strong;
Victor and vanquished equally may win[10],
Climbing far heights, where fame, eternal fame,
White as the gleaming cloak of Arctic hills,
Rests as a mantle, fadeless, faultless, pure, 170
On loftiest lives, whose snowy peaks, sun-crowned,
Receive but to dispense their blessedness.

"Eternal life demands a selfless love.
Hampered by pride, greed, hate, what soul can grow[11]?
Conceive a selfish God! Thou canst not, man!
Then let it shame thee unto higher things.
Who strives for self hates other men's success;
Who seeks God's glory welcomes rivalry.
Seeking, not gift, but Giver, thou shalt find
No sacrifice but changes part for whole. 180

"Fare on, full sure that greatest glory comes,
And swiftest growth, from serving humankind.
Toil on, for toil is treasure, thine for aye;
A pauper he who boasts an empty name."

So spake the Spirit of the Infinite[12].
The Messenger and Mind of Holy Twain.

Some men I found embodiments of all
The goodness, all the greatness, I had dreamed;
Men seeming gods, bestowing benefits
As suns their beams, as seas and skies their showers. 190
Others as dwarfs, as despots, by compare,
Devoured with greed, consumed with jealousy.

But truth taught charity, gave me to see,
As face to face one sees familiar friend,
Why men are not alike in magnitude.

Some souls, than others, have more summits climbed,
More light absorbed, more moral might evolved.
Dowered are they with wealth from earlier spheres;
Hence wiser, worthier, than those they lead
Through precept's vale, up steep example's height, 200
To where love, beauty, wealth, power, glory, reign.

   While some, innately noble, are borne down
By weight of weaknesses inherited,
By passions fierce, propensities depraved,
Malific legacy of centuries,
That much of their true worthiness obscures,
While spirit strives with flesh for mastery,
For higher culture and for added might.

   And yet anon such souls effulgent shine—
As bursts the April beam through banks of cloud— 210
In glory from which envy shades its eyes,
While stands detraction staring, stricken dumb;
The glory of a great intelligence,
Which mortal mists can dim but for a time.

   Spirits, like stars, still differ in degree,
And cannot show an even excellence,
Unequal in their first nobility.
Great tells of greater—littleness of less;
Time's hills and vales[13] but type eternity.

   Truth taught me more, but bade me silent be; 220
And I had teachers else—toil, prayer, and pain,
With days and nights of misery's martyrdom,
Alone and lorn in grief's Gethsemane:
Till storm above, and earthquake underneath,
Shook down thought's prison house, broke bolt and bar,
And agony set inspiration free.

   'Tis thus the Great Musician tunes the harp
That He would strike—strikes thus the harp in tune;
Sweeping with sorrow's hand the quivering strings,
That they may cry aloud, and haply sound 230
A loftier and more enduring lay.

CANTO TWO

The Soul of Song[1]

 Alone my soul upon a mighty hill,
Ancient with lingering snows of vanished years,
Where towering forms the templed azure fill,
Wooed by the breath of woodland atmospheres;
Where Nature, throned in solitude, reveres
The God whose glory she doth symbolize,
And on these altars, watered by her tears,
Spreads far around the fragrant sacrifice
Whose incense wafts her sweet memorial to the skies. 240

 Here will I rest, where I have loved to roam,
From childhood's rose-hued, scarce-remembered day,
And found my pensive soul's congenial home
Far from the depths where human passions play.
Born at their feet, my own have learned to stray
Familiar o'er these pathless heights, and feel,
As now, the mind assume a loftier sway,
Soaring for themes that o'er its summits steal,
Beyond all thought to reach, all utterance to reveal.

 Here let me linger. O my native hills! 250
Solemn and watchful o'er the silent waste!
How great the joy his bounding bosom thrills,
Whose steps, aspiring, mar your summits chaste!
Language! thy richest robe, thy rarest taste,
How clothe description in befitting dress,
When halts imagination's wingéd haste,
Awe-spelled in wonder's conscious littleness,
Where loom the cloud-crowned monarchs of the wilderness?

 Grim, storm-plumed guardians! Warriors tempest-mailed,
Federal with freedom, fortressing her land! 260
Had primal man the sacred garden[2] tilled,
'Ere earthly scenes your early vision scanned?
In spirit form took ye your titan stand[3],
Ere rolled a world-creating fiat forth?
Or came ye at convulsion's fierce command,
'Mid loud-tongued thunders bursting from the earth,
The martial music that proclaimed your war-like birth?

    Vast, voiceless oracles, whose intelligence
Sleeps in the caverns of each stony heart,
Yet breathes o'er all a boundless eloquence, 270
What wealth historic might your words impart!
Lone, looming, hermit of the hills, apart
From where thy banded mates in union dwell!
A master lyrist seemingly thou art,
Chief harper of a host that round thee swell;
And thine the Orphean boon[4], what could withstand thy spell?

    E'en now it whispers from the graven rock,
Scribed with the lightning's pen, in sculpture bold,
Defying time and tide and tempest shock,
Frowning where seas and centuries have rolled. 280
"Oh were my words[5] thus writ!" That sage of old,
Knew he not well, ye mighty tomes of clay,
How firm the trust your flinty page might hold?
Have ye not scorned the fiats of decay?
Are ye not standing now where nations passed away?

    Thrice wondrous things, once thine to wisely scan,
Fast as thy frozen snow-crown, still in store,
Hadst thou the melting gift[6]—of sovereign man
The sunlike glory—mightest thou restore,
Till learning's tide o'erwhelmed the shining shore, 290
With rich revealings of lost realms that rose
And fell like frost-hewn flowers thy face before;
Blightings which brought them an untimely close—
Perchance, of spirit lore, some mystic mine disclose.

    But like the laboring brain that burns to speak
Mind's inmost thought, in deepest dungeon pent;
Or liker still to inward boiling peak
Of fires volcanic, vainly seeking vent
Where adamantine bolts and bars prevent;—
Thou'rt doomed to utter stillness, and shalt keep 300
The burden of thy bearing till is rent
Yon heavenly veil, and earth and air and deep
Tell secrets that shall rouse the dead from solemn sleep.

    And must I be as mute, O silent mount!
Muse of all Melody, shall I not sing?—
Burst these dumb bars, when e'en yon babbling fount
May find in every breeze a wafting wing,
Afar its lightest murmured word to fling?

    Where art thou, ancient Soul of Solemn Song?
    Asleep? Then wake! Wherefore art slumbering? 310
    The world hath need of thee, and waiteth long.
Strike, strike again thy harp, and thrill the listening throng!

      Thus musing, lone upon a beetling brow,
    Quaffing from unseen fount, those wilds among,
    The spirit of the sun-kissed torrent flow,
    Methought some lofty, caverned cliff had rung
    With echoings of a more than mortal tongue;
    Though softly clear the mournful cadence broke,
    As notes from off the weird-toned viol flung.
    Or was it yon lone cloud that muttering spoke, 320
Heralding the storm king's wrathful shout and shivering stroke?

      Amazed I listened. Did I more than dream?
    Had random word aroused unhoped reply?
    Or was it sound whose import did but seem?
    Hark!—for again it rolls along the sky:
    "Then question hast thou none? Or none wouldst ply,
    Save to thy soul in meditative strain,
    Or heedless winds that wander idly by?
    So be it; still to me thy purpose plain,
Thy hidden wish revealed, nor thus revealed in vain." 330

      While freshening waves of woodland-scented air
    Widened the spell of that immortal tone;
    While, as on threshold of a lion's lair,
    Speechless I stood, as stricken into stone;
    Methought the sun with lessening splendor shone,
    As if that wandering cloud obscured his gaze.
    Then burst the glory from his midday throne!
    Turning, mine eye beheld, in rapt amaze,
What memory ne'er would lose were life of endless days.

      A stately form, of giant stature tall; 340
    Of hoary aspect, venerable and grave;
    Whose curling locks and beard of copious fall
    Vied the white foam of ocean's storm-whipt wave.
    The firm-fixt eye flashed lightnings from its cave;
    Far-darting penetration's gaze combined
    With wisdom's milder light. Of study gave
    Deep evidence that brow by learning lined,
Thought's towering throne, where ruled his realm a monarch
    mind.

    The spirit's garb—for spirit so he seemed— 350
Fell radiant in many a flowing fold;
A robe antique, by modern limners deemed
Befitting monk or eremite of old.
Head, hands, and feet were bare; the presence bold
With majesty, e'en as a god might wear,
While condescending to a mortal mould.
He spake—the voice no longer thrilled with fear;
Like some vast organ swell, it charmed, enchained, the ear.

    "Long have I watched and waited, but no sound
Broke the wild stillness of this stern abode, 360
Save thunder's fiery foot-print smote the ground,
Or far beneath some torrent's fury flowed;
Anon the screaming eagle past me rode;
The seeker after gold, with toilsome stride,
And eager eye to fix the shining lode,
Hath paused and panted on the hill's steep side;
But none, for greater things, till now have hither hied.

    "And thou, O pensive crier in the waste,
Invoker of the Voice now visible!
Prepared art thou a mystery to taste, 370
Whose fruit is joy or woe ineffable?
Pluck not of wisdom's branches bending full,
Drink not of that divine philosophy,
Save thou canst bravely suffer wrong's misrule,
Thy best intent thought ill; save thou canst be
What men deem "fool," real fools despising, pitying thee.

    "Not all my ministry to lift the gloom
Yet hovering o'er this mystic hemisphere.
List while I tell, for I am one by whom
Future and past as present shall appear. 380
In me behold Messiah's Minister,
Ancient of time and of eternity,
Spirit of song that moved the Hebrew seer,
Voice of the stars[7] ere earth's nativity;
Exile, for ages gone, of mortal minstrelsy.

    "See now my sacred heritage, the prey
Of ribald rhymesters, sensuous, half obscene;
Of gloating censors, glad o'er my decay,
And deeming all but best I ne'er had been!
The body's bard[8] throned, sceptering the scene, 390

A groveling worshiper of earth and time.
Arise! and with thy soul's celestial sheen,
Shame these false meteors, change the ruling chime;
My minstrel, I thy muse, sing thou the song sublime!

"Sing, poet, sing! but not of new—of old,
Of old and new—eternal truth thy theme,
That holdeth past and future in her fold,
That maketh present but a passing dream,
While time and earth and man as trifles seem;
That knoweth not of new, or old, or strange; 400
Whose everduring, all-redemptive scheme,
Fixt and immutable 'mid worlds of change,
On, on, from universe to universe doth range.

"Faint not, nor fear, for all shall fare thy way—
My way, His way, the Master's, evermore.
East shall seem West, rethrown the rising ray,
Shining afar from this most ancient shore[9],
And man shall rise[10] e'en where man fell before.
Fools may deride, may jeer at destiny;
They mock to mourn, oblivion earths them o'er; 410
While they that champion truth, by truth shall be
Exalted, e'en in time, to live eternally."

The ancient paused, and, unperceived till then,
A wondrous harp his bosom swung before,
Such harp as played the shepherd psalmist[11] when
A maddening rage his monarch seized and tore,
And music's magic quelled satanic power.
Seated, his form against the crag reclined,
He waved me to his feet, and forth did pour,
As pours Niagara on the plaintive wind, 420
Floods of majestic song, falling from mind to mind.

Full tale of wonders told, I may not tell,
Though mind be heir to all of mystery;
With milk of truth the breasts of wisdom swell,
Sufficing past and present infancy.
But matching all the modern eye may see
With marvels promised to the future sight,
'Twas as the shrub unto the sheltering tree,
The floating swan unto the eagle's flight,
The hillock to the snow-crowned summit, lost in light. 430

Silent he towered above me, harp in hand,—
Was it a dream? Could dream so vivid be?—
And with his mantle's fold my forehead fanned.
Then leapt to life the flame of poesy!
Was it a vision of my destiny?
Upon the mount, as erst, I stood alone,
And naught was there of muse or minstrelsy;
Save that afar still trembled that strange tone,
And something said within: "That harp is now thine own."

CANTO THREE

Elect of Elohim[1]

 Sing I a song of aeons gone, 440
 Of life from mystery sprung,
Ere sun, or moon, or rolling stars
 Their radiance earthward flung;
Ere spirit-winged intelligence
 Forsook those shining spheres.
Exceeding glory there to gain
 Through mortal toil and tears.

 A song they learn whose lives eterne
 Transcend yon twinkling night,
Pale Olea's silver beam[2] outsoar, 450
 Shinea's golden flight;
Passing the angel sentries by,
 Mounting o'er stars and suns,
To where the orbs that govern burn,
 Royal and regnant ones.

 Declare, O Muse of mightier wing,
 Of loftier lore, than mine!
Why God is God, and man may be
 Both human and divine;
Why Sons of God, 'mid sons of men, 460
 Unrecognized may dwell,
So masked in dense mortality
 That none their truth can tell.

 From worlds afar, from heavenmost star,
 Heard I, or seemed to hear,
A sweet refrain, as summer rain,
 A cadence soft and clear.
A voice, a harp,—Was it the same?—
 Harping those harps among,
Leading the lyric universe, 470
 On those high hills of song?

 In solemn council sat the Gods;
 From Kolob's height supreme,
Celestial light blazed forth afar
 O'er countless kokaubeam;
And faintest tinge, the fiery fringe

Of that resplendent day,
'Lumined the dark abysmal realm
   Where earth in chaos lay.

   Silence. That awful hour was one 480
   When thought doth most avail;
Of worlds unborn the destiny
   Hung trembling in the scale.
Silence self-spelled, and there arose,
   Those kings and priests among,
A power sublime, than whom appeared
   None nobler 'mid the throng.

   A stature mingling strength with grace,
   Of meek though godlike mien;
The glory of whose countenance 490
   Outshone the noonday sheen.
Whiter his hair than ocean spray,
   Or frost of alpine hill.
He spake;—attention grew more grave,
   The stillness e'en more still.

   "Father!" the voice like music fell,
   Clear as the murmuring flow
Of mountain streamlet trickling down
   From heights of virgin snow.
"Father," it said, "since one must die, 500
   Thy children to redeem
From spheres all formless now and void,
   Where pulsing life shall teem;

   "And mighty Michael[3] foremost fall,
   That mortal man may be;
And chosen saviour Thou must send,
   Lo, here am I—send me!
I ask, I seek no recompense,
   Save that which then were mine;
Mine be the willing sacrifice, 510
   The endless glory Thine!

   "Give me to lead to this lorn world,
   When wandered from the fold,
Twelve legions of the noble ones
   That now Thy face behold;
Tried souls[4], 'mid untried spirits found,
   That captained these may be,

And crowned the dispensations all
   With powers of Deity.

"Who blameless bide the spirit state, 520
   Clothe them in mortal clay,
The stepping-stone[5] to glories all,
   If man will God obey,
Believing where he cannot see,
   Till he again shall know,
And answer give, reward receive,
   For all deeds done below.

"The love that hath redeemed all worlds[6]
   All worlds must still redeem;
But mercy cannot justice rob— 530
   Or where were Elohim?
Freedom—man's faith, man's work, God's grace—
   Must span the great gulf o'er;
Life, death, the guerdon or the doom,
   Rejoice we or deplore."

   Still rang that voice, when sudden rose
     Aloft a towering form,
Proudly erect as lowering peak
   'Lumed by the gathering storm;
A presence bright and beautiful, 540
   With eye of flashing fire,
A lip whose haughty curl bespoke
   A sense of inward ire.

   "Send me!"—coiled 'neath his courtly smile
     A scarce concealed disdain—
"And none shall hence, from heaven to earth,
   That shall not rise again.
My saving plan exception scorns[7].
   Man's will?—Nay, mine alone.
As recompense, I claim the right 550
   To sit on yonder Throne!"

   Ceased Lucifer. The breathless hush
     Resumed and denser grew.
All eyes were turned; the general gaze
   One common magnet drew.
A moment there was solemn pause—
   Listened eternity,

While rolled from lips omnipotent
    The Father's firm decree:

    "Jehovah, thou my Messenger[8]! 560
        Son Ahman, thee I send;
And one shall go thy face before,[9]
    While twelve thy steps attend.
And many more on that far shore
    The pathway shall prepare,
That I, the first, the last may come,
    And earth my glory share.

    "After and ere thy going down,
        An army shall descend—
The host of God, and house of him 570
    Whom I have named my friend[10].
Through him, upon Idumea[11],
    Shall come, all life to leaven,
The guileless ones, the sovereign sons,
    Throned on the heights of heaven.

    "Go forth, thou Chosen of the Gods,
        Whose strength shall in thee dwell!
Go down betime and rescue earth,
    Dethroning death and hell.
On thee alone man's fate depends, 580
    The fate of beings all.
Thou shalt not fail, though thou art free—
    Free, but too great to fall.

    "By arm divine, both mine and thine,
        The lost thou shalt restore,
And man, redeemed, with God shall be,
    As God forevermore.
Return, and to the parent fold
    This wandering planet bring[12],
And earth shall hail thee Conqueror, 590
    And heaven proclaim thee King."

    'Twas done. From congregation vast,
        Tumultuous murmurs rose;
Waves of conflicting sound, as when
    Two meeting seas oppose.
'Twas finished. But the heavens wept;
    And still their annals tell

How one was choice of Elohim,
    O'er one who fighting fell.

—-

A stranger star that came from far 600
    To fling its silver ray,
Where, cradled in a lowly cave,
    A lowlier infant lay;
And led by soft sidereal light,
    The orient sages bring
Bare gifts of gold and frankincense,
    To greet the homeless King.

O wondrous grace! Will gods go down
    Thus low that men may rise?
Imprisoned here the Mighty One, 610
    Who reigned in yonder skies?
Hark to that chime!—What tongue sublime
    Now tells the hour of noon[13]?
O dying world! art welcoming
    Life's life—Light's sun and moon[14]?

Proclaim Him, prophet harbinger!
    Make plain the Mightier's way,
Thou sharer of His martyrdom!
    Elias? Yea and Nay[15].
The crescent moon, that knew the Sun, 620
    Ere stars had learned to shine[16];
The waning moon, that bathed in blood,
    Ere sank the Sun divine.

"Glory to God!—good will to man!—
    Peace, peace!"—triumphal tone.
"Why peace?" Is discord then no more?
    Are earth and heaven as one?
Peace to the soul that serveth Him,
    The monarch manger-born;
There, ruler of unnumbered realms; 630
    Here, throneless and forlorn.

He wandered through the faithless world,
    A prince in shepherd guise;
He called his scattered flock, but few
    The Voice did recognize;
For minds upborne by hollow pride,

  Or dimmed by sordid lust,
Ne'er look for kings in beggar's garb,
  For diamonds in the dust.

  Wept He above a city doomed[17], 640
  Her temple, walls, and towers,
O'er palaces where recreant priests
  Usurped unhallowed powers.
"I am the way, the life, the light!"
  Alas! 'twas heeded not.
Ignored—nay, mocked—God scorned by man!—
  And spurned the truth He taught.

  O bane of damning unbelief!
  When, when till now so rife?
Thou stumbling stone, thou barrier 'thwart 650
  The gates of endless life!
O love of self, and mammon lust,
  Twin portals to despair,
Where bigotry, the blinded bat,
  Flaps through the midnight air!

  Through these, gloom-wrapt Gethsemane[18]!
  Thy glens of guilty shade
Grieved o'er the sinless Son of God,
  By gold-bought kiss betrayed;
Beheld Him unresisting dragged, 660
  Forsaken, friendless, lone,
To halls where dark-browed hatred sat
  On judgment's lofty throne.

  As sheep before His shearers, dumb,
  Those patient lips were mute;
The clamorous charge of taunting tongues
  He deigned not to dispute.
They smote with cruel palm a face
  Which felt yet bore the sting;
Then crowned with thorns His quivering brow, 670
  And, mocking, hailed him "King!"

  Transfixt He hung,—O crime of crimes!—
  The God whom worlds adore.
"Father forgive them!" Drained the dregs;
  Immanuel[19]—no more.
No more where thunders shook the earth,
  Where lightnings tore the gloom,

Saw that unconquered Spirit spurn
   The shackles of the tomb.

   Far-flaming might, a sword of light, 680
   A falchion from its sheath,
It cleft the realms of darkness, and
   Dissolved the bands of death.
Hell's dungeons burst, wide open swung
   The everlasting bars,
Whereby the ransomed soul shall win
   Those heights beyond the stars.

CANTO FOUR

Night And The Wilderness[1]

A World o'ershadowed by an Eagle's wings[2],
From Scythian snows to hot Hamitic sands,
From Ganges on to Tiber and the Thames. 690

Where goeth forth, unwittingly the tool
Of Truth Eterne, a pathway to prepare,
The law and legion of imperial Rome,
Mighty to crush and to consolidate,
Humbling the hard, the haughty, making way
For peace to flow[3] wider than war can wound
Servant unknowingly of Him she slew,
In pandering to Judah's jealousy.

Victim now Victor, conqueror captive led,
Debtor to justice, darkness serving day, 700
Upon her knotted neck Jehovah's heel,
Her iron hand the Nazarene's defense,
Holding in quell the hierarchal hate,
Curbing the cruel wrath of Greek and Jew;
Israel from Israel's madness made secure—
Lamb from the Lion, by the She-Wolf's might[4].

Ere rose the Iron-Limbed[5], all conquering,
Throned on the wreck of empires earlier born,
Wrought well for Him the brazen loin of power,
The pard-like phalanx, swift, invincible, 710
Spreading the glories of a sapient tongue,
The wing whereon a higher wisdom flew,
Till teemed, of Aryan clans, the Asian kin[6],
Seedlings of Japheth, sire of the Gentile world.
Soul-widening word, broad-sown by Grecia's hand,
To blossom on a furrowed heathen ground.

Servant, erstwhile, the silver-breasted realm,
Kingdom of Kurush[7], shepherd of the King,
Whose sword, that gave the Jew deliverance,
To golden Babylon the guillotine. 720

Whoe'er hath swayed, or yet shall sway, the world,
By tongue or pen, by sword or sceptered rule,
Hath served, or yet shall serve, the sovereign aim
Of Him who wills the welfare of mankind;

For or against, promoting still His plan,
Helping, not hindering, a conquering Cause.

   Gone the great Sun—set but to rise again,
More glorious from a night of martyrdom;
Set here to rise on realms and times untold;
All worlds, God's lofty vineyards[8], visiting. 730

   Linger the spirit Moon and speaking Stars[9],
Crowning with light the Woman Wonderful[10].

   Fair as the morn, though tearful as the eve;
Risen as from the rocky sepulchre,
Where slept betimes the body of her Lord;
Clothed, crowned, and shod, with glory's symboling[11];
Ere winging to the vast invisible,
Returning to the restful wilderness,
She bides to hope, to labor, and endure,
All depths, all heights, with Him inheriting. 740

   Henceforth with her another Comforter,
Vicegerent[12] of the vanished Majesty,
Of heavenly Three, the unembodied One[13],
Proceeding from the presence of the Sire,
To manifest the meaning of the Son;
Giver of gifts from Him, the glory-crowned,
Fountain of memory and of prophecy.

   After and ere,[14] Messiah's Minister,
Creative hand, omnific arm of God;
Holder with Christ of resurrection's key, 750
The quickener of the living and the dead.
Lamp of the worlds, life of the universe,
Eternal spring of energy divine—
Life, Light, and Love, magnetic mystery,
Whereby all things upheld and heavenward drawn.

   Prophet still pleading[15] in the wilderness,
The promise of a perfect yet to come;
Proclaimer of the heavenly commonweal,
Kingdom upon and yet not of the earth,
Whose portal none can enter, none can see, 760
Save born anew—born of a dual birth,
By mystic fatherhood and motherhood
Begotten sons and daughters unto God,
Whose Spirit, omnipresent, immanent,

Unwearied, strives by countless ministries,
By might of word, by miracle of deed,
Mankind to win, wooing while hope remains.

    Henceforth with her that holy gift and guide,
Truth's high revealer and interpreter;
Henceforth with her the Father and the Son, 770
Absent, yet present by the Comforter;
Of great lights twain, the lesser, ruling night,
Moon to that Sun, whose realm the rounded Day.

    Resplendent night, while flame those fluent stars[16],
That still a spotless brow bediadem;
Circling forever round their central Light,
And, Him withdrawn, repeating from afar,
And gladdening with His rays a gloom-hung world.

    As set that Sun, sinking in seas of blood,
Sinking to soar above a mightier morrow, 780
Follow the lingering stars, save haply one[17],
Through mystic night of ages sparkling lone,
And speaking in high splendor things to come.
Most lustrous of the living lamps of God,
'Mid human lights, divinely luminant.
Rarest of twelve, remaining oracle,
Reserved unto a wondrous destiny;
Pilot of peoples, nations, tribes and tongues,
Leading the lost[18] ones from captivity.
Beloved of Love—life's King, death's Conqueror, 790
Tarrying by will of Him through troubled time,
Lighting the way unto eternity.

    And thou, e'en thou, O Woman Wonderful!
Safe for a season from the She-Wolf's maw,
Far borne, cast, west, on power's imperial wings,
Nourished 'neath Caesar's shield, till Caesar's sword
Hath turned upon and made thee desolate.
Thou too must pass—not perish—in thy time.
Betrayed to foes without, by false within,
E'en as thy Lord thou sufferest martyrdom. 800

    But what avails to baffle Him or bind?
Vain, dragon, vain thy deluge of deceit,
Thy flood of lies, thou false one from of old!
Vain, wrath of devils and of men combined,
Bent to defile the sacred Bride of Christ.

Triumphs the Man-Child[19], heaven now summons home;
Triumphs the Woman in the wilderness,
'Scaping the jaws, the hungering gates of hell,
That 'gainst the mortal part alone prevail;
Body, not spirit, crushed and all o'ercome. 810

   Throned upon higher worlds, she reigneth still;
And here shall rise unto the regnant place,
When rolls the stone upon the image doomed,
When God hath fanned with fire His threshing floor.

   Till then proud Japheth sways[20], while Jacob mourns,
Fainting 'neath yokes and fardels, prostrate, prone,
With Judah undermost, the last of all
The trampled tribes to taste of liberty.
Haply ordained a lesser power to wield,
Antaeus-like[21], from touching of the ground; 820
Bent, curst, yet clutching, and by might of gold
Conquering his dust-adoring conqueror[22].

   For God, through all, remembers Abraham,
Ordained of old His lineal house to be.
Came not the Christ their covenant to fulfill?
Who but an Israel might offer Him?
Whose hand than Judah's might Jehovah slay?
"His blood be on our head"—Ay, rests it there!
Weightier than worlds by that high death redeemed.

   World-wandering Saul! Was this thy symboling: 830
The Jew struck blind that Gentile hosts might see[23]?

   Predestined Israel, martyred, immolate[24],
That nations, blood-besprent, might look and live;
A burden-bearer for the universe,
Outcast and homeless for humanity,
Descending like his Lord all else below,
And yet with Him to rise all else above,
Extremes of woe and weal encompassing,
Wisdom by sweet and bitter made more wise.

   From blight springs blessing, and from darkness day; 840
E'en Canaan's neck from 'neath the yoke[25] shall come.
Japheth shall feel the Spirit minister,
And Jacob see and hear his risen Lord[26].

   Departed now the Woman Wonderful,
Gone with the spirit gift and guiding power;

O'ercome, world-conquered, sinks degenerate
The washed one to his wallowing in the mire[27];
A drowsy dreamer of the self-same dreams
Dispelled erewhile by lightnings of her eye;

    The heaven-lit torch[28] that made the pathway plain 850
O'er rugged mount, through mazy catacomb,
Now dimmed with incense from Diana's shrine[29],
And dashed in pieces 'gainst a pagan throne,
Where prematurely changed was cross for crown,
And Christ's flock fleeced by shearing compromise[30].

    God still with man, though not with man's misrule;
Still with the just, though Christian-pagan turn
His prurient ear to fables, from the truth,
And, virtueless as Judah's pharisee,
And graceless as Iscariot, self-hung, 860
Parts in the midst, as wide as East from West[31],
False church and faithless empire, faction-torn,
Twain as the imaged legs of Babel's dream,
A split colossus, fallen 'twixt Greece and Rome.

    God still with man, though not with man's misrule,
Never with thee, daughter of force and fraud,
Mother of guile—thy refuge and thy shame!
Never with thee, thou wanton by the way,
Roaming tradition's tangled wilderness,
Lost in a night that seemeth to thee day; 870
In crooked paths that fain would straight appear;
Warming thy withered fingers o'er the coals
Alive 'mid ashes of the ancient fires,
Where She was wont[32] to kindle faith, hope, love,
And flash the beacon o'er a wandering world.
There holding to thy heart an empty urn,
There cherishing a name, a memory,
Mumbling vain prayers, "Lord, Lord," protesting still,
And still forgetful of thy Lord's command!

    Nay, not with thee, thou crimson courtesan[33], 880
Robed in the horrid hue of countless crimes!
Fierce dragon's maw, thrice-cruel murderess,
Thy hands a-reek with blood of innocence,
With blood of prophets, blood of priests and kings,
Whose martyred souls sue vengeance, judgment-sworn!
Vengeance on thee, thou slaughterer of saints,

Vengeance on him, thy sceptered paramour,
Whose princes ten (while Mammon's host shall wail),
Loathing where once they loved all lustfully,
And lived, as thou hast lived, deliciously, 890
When found no more God's wheat 'mid Satan's tares,
When thou art saltless, saintless, savorless,
When thou art ripened unto rottenness,
Shall give thy crumbling body to be burned.

   Nay, Anti-Christ, presuming tyranny,
Never with thee, usurping power of sin!
Plotting to sway Jehovah's sovereignty,
To rear thy throne where His alone shall stand;
Perdition, warring 'gainst the Saints of God,
And overcoming till the Judgment sits[34], 900
When swift-winged morn shall overtake the night,
And glory lift the gloom[35] of centuries.

   Meanwhile the mission of the Moonlike One[36],
Brooding above the waters of the world,
Stronger than storms, mightier than wind or wave,
Moving on mortal seas, on human souls;
Dynamic impulse of Divinity,
Impelling to all action[37] wise, sublime.

   That high Ambassador of Elohim,
The Spirit Messenger Omnipotent, 910
Declare His goings-forth, His sendings tell.

   Ye patriarchs and prophets of old time!
Ye seers and bards of sacred Israel!
Elect of God, earth-wandering witnesses,
Sowers on goodly and on stony ground!
Souls mercy-sent, man's erring steps to win
From folly's paths of wickedness and strife,
To wisdom's way of purity and peace!
Shepherds to fold and feed a wolf-torn flock,
Holding the hallowed keys that loose and bind! 920
Tell me—are ye alone truth's harbingers?
Are ye alone forerunners of the Light?

   Nay, for as kings and conquerors they come;
Anon, as champions of democracy;
Founders of faiths and stern iconoclasts;
Sword, tongue and pen of progress and reform.
The fountain lights of literature, whose rays

Spill their white splendor on the hills of fame;
Masters of melody, whose strains awake
The slumbering memories of eternity; 930
Pilgrims to continents and climes unknown,
Uncurtained for the play of liberty,
Now nearing the finale of her dreams,
Dreams that shall waken to reality;
Waste-winners; probers of the polar way;
Invention's wizards, wielding magic might—
Launching fleet words on atmospheric wave,
Cleaving with bird-like wing the shoreless blue,
Outspeeding speed, outblazing brilliancy,
Thrilling the world with lightning's vivid wand, 940
Ruling all realms with scintillating sway;
Sages in art, in science past profound,
Subduing matter and exploring mind,
Sounding the depths of psychic mystery,
Scaling thought's pinnacles, that pierce the night,
To greet the early glintings of the morn.
These also are the mighty, kin to those,
Divinest of Jehovah's messengers.
Each hath his freedom, and succeeds or fails,
But all subserve the Will Omnipotent. 950

   What though some wayward son of Deity[38],
Builder, o'erthrower, of imperial thrones,
In wrongful act of rightful agency,
Here drench with blood, here pave with shattered bones,
To heights of crumbling power and futile fame!
Is God then mocked? Made void His vast design?
Creator foiled by creature? Vain the fear!
Speeds ne'er to earth a spoiler of His plan,
Nor spares His rod a recreant messenger.

   Whate'er betide, the soul that sins atones: 960
The grievous sceptre and the slaughtering sword,
The bloodstained ax, the gory guillotine,
The tyrant wrong, the tyrant-trampling right,
Join to make justice of the direst doom.

   All oracles of light, all arms of power,
Preparers of the way one face before;
Their strength but part of His omnipotence,
Their fault God-given lest man be deified,
And pride in him dethrone humility.

    Declare His truth, His generations tell, 970
O'er whom the many marveled, some to say
Elias, slain of Herod, lives again;
While some said Jeremias[39]. Who say ye,
Man-hated, though God-missioned ministers,
Unctioned with fire, anointed from on High!
Guardians yet watchful o'er the widening fold!
Who say ye was your Master, Teacher, Friend?

    "Word that was God, is God, and shall be aye;
Sire by the spirit, and by flesh the Son;
In glory with the Father ere the world, 980
And now with that same glory glorified.
Image and likeness of creation's cause,
Mirror and model of humanity[40],
Of man the parent and the prototype.
Lover of light, hating and righting wrong;
Anointed Lord of Lords and Sire 'mid Sons;
The Sole-begotten, He that doeth here
All He hath seen erstwhile the Father do.
Elias? Nay, Messiah, Saviour, King,
That Greater whom Elias said would come." 990

    Sufficeth it. What now, ye learned ones,
School-taught, self-sent, man-missioned ministers,
Creators of a vain divinity!
Daring the thunders of the decalogue,
Disputing Moses, Christ, and prophets all,
Gird up your loins and answer—What of God?
"God?—Mystery incomprehensible[41];
All things made He from nothing"—Hold, enough!
Night and gross darkness—darken it no more.

    Yet give to man his meed. Hath he not kept, 1000
Albeit in empty urn, the Name of Names,
And toiled and suffered sore transmitting it
From sire to son through shaded centuries?
Messiah's coming did he not proclaim?
And, trodden yet beneath oppression's heel,
Hoards he not still the precious prophecy?
The Jew, the Christian, each hath played his part,
Each as a star[42] hath heralded a morn.

    And what of him, the fierce iconoclast,
Agnostic, doubting or denying all, 1010

Ofttimes in hate and horrid ribaldry?
Maintains he not life's equilibrium,
A tempering shadow to the torrid beam,
A brake upon the wheel of bigotry,
A jet to cool fanaticism's flame,
Unquelled, devouring, devastating all?
An angel, past control, a demon were.
Bold unbelief, reform's rough pioneer,
Unwittingly a warrior for the Cross,
A weapon for the right[43] he ridicules. 1020

   God's perfect plan an ocean is, where range
As minnows, monsters, of the wide wave-realm,
Men's causes, creeds, and systems manifold;
Free as the will of Him who freedom willed,
Within the bounds ordained by law divine.
E'en Lucifer, arch-foe to liberty,
Is free, though fettered to his fallen sphere;
Enticing, tempting all, compelling none,
And aiding aye the Power he fain would foil.

   All human schemes, all hell's conspiracies, 1030
All chance, all accident, all agency,
All loves, hates, hopes, despairs, and blasphemies,
All rights, all wrongs, to one high purpose bend.
No backward glance gives progress. Upward! on!
Life triumphs ever in death's victory.
Dross hath its ministry no less than gold;
And honest, erring zeal, wherever found,
Hath wrought more good than ill to humankind.

   But morn must rise, and night dismiss her stars;
And ocean summon home his seas and streams; 1040
And truth the perfect, truth the part fulfill,
As knowledge faith, as history prophecy.

   Day from his quiver drew a shining shaft,
And 'thwart the night the flaming arrow flew.
Hark, to a cry that cleaves the wilderness,
Pealing the clarion prelude to the dawn!

CANTO FIVE

The Messenger of Morn[1]

"Wake, slumbering world! Vain dreamer, dream no more!
The shadows lift, and o'er night's dusky beach
Ripple the white waves of morn. Awake! Arise!

"Ocean of dispensations—rivers, rills, 1050
Roll to your source! End, to thine origin!
And Israel, to the rock whence ye were hewn[2]!
For He that scattered, gathereth His flock,
His ancient flock, and plants their pilgrim feet
On Joseph's mountain top and Judah's plains;
Recalls the children of the covenant
From long dispersion o'er the Gentile world,
Mingling their spirits with the mystic sea,
Which sent them forth as freshening showers to save
The parched and withered wastes of unbelief[3]. 1060
Japheth! thy planet pales[4], it sinks, it sets;
Henceforth 't is Jacob's star must rise and reign.

"Daughter of Zion! be thou comforted,
And wash from thy wan cheek all trace of tears.
Gone are the days of dole and widowhood,
The days of barrenness that brought thee scorn;
Thy wilderness now weds, thy desert blooms.

"Rejoice, Jerusalem! thou art redeemed;
Again thy temple and thy towers arise;
Heard is the harp of David in thy halls; 1070
Greater than Solomon's thy wisdom shines.

"From spirit heights, where thou art beautiful,
Lamp of the nations, send thy light afar!
Take on thy new name—One and Pure in Heart!
For thou shalt see thy God, His presence thine.

"Time, mighty daughter of Eternity!
Mother of centuries[5]—seventy, seven-crowned!
Assemble now thy children at thy side,
And 'ere thou diest teach them to be one[6].
Link to its link rebind the broken chain 1080
Of dispensations, glories, keys, and powers,
From Adam's fall unto Messiah's reign;

A thousand years of rest, a day with God,
While Shiloh reigns[7] and Kolob once revolves.

    "Six days thou, Earth, hast labored[8], and the seventh,
Thy sabbath, comes apace! Night's sceptre wanes,
And in the East the silvery Messenger
Gives silent token of the golden Dawn.

    "Once more the ancient tidings[9] among men!
Once more the sign and seal of heavenly power! 1090
Renewal of an endless covenant,
Elias, restitution, unity!

    "His burden! Hear it, nations! Hear it, isles!
Ere falls an hour, night's darkest hour of doom.
The trial ends, the judgment now begins.
Out, out of her, my people, saith your God!"

    Who towers aloft, as mountain girt with hills,
Amid the strength of Ephraim's stalwart sons,
To trumpet thus the closing acts of time?
Speak, oracle, what sayest thou of thyself? 1100
Who art thou, man of might and majesty?

    "Would God I might but tell thee who I am!
Would God I might but tell thee what I know[10]!"

    Then was he of the Mighty—one with those
Descended from the Empire of the Sun,
Adown the glowing stairway of the stars?
Regnant and ruling ere they left the realms
Of life supernal, left their sovereign thrones,
To wander oft as outcasts of mankind,
Unknown, unhonored, e'en like One who came 1110
Unto His own, by them spat on and spurned?
Avails it aught, their name or nation here?
Their state and standing there, the vital tale.

    Peers of that Empire, nobles of the skies,
The sceptered satraps of the King of Kings,
The royal retinue of Him who reigns
First-born of many brethren—Gibborim[11],
Great ones worthy the Word[12] that was to come;
Foreknown, elect, predestined, preordained,
Sons of the Gods, and saviours of mankind, 1120

Building the highway for Messiah's feet,
And wheresoe'er He fareth following.

    I saw in vision such a one descend,
And garb him in a guise of common clay;
His glory veiling from the gaze of all,
Who wist not that a great one walked with men;
Nor knew it then the soul incarnate there,
Betwixt the temporal and spirit spheres
So dense forgetfulness doth intervene;
Yet learned his truth betime by angel tongues, 1130
By voice of God, by heavenly whisperings.

    But who remains his mystery to solve,
His letter to unlock with spirit key?
The veil to lift by death and silence thrown
O'er all the splendors of that life sublime?

    Sound, Angel, sound! thou fifth of seven[13], ordained
To usher in the world-millennials,
To storm the dungeon doors of history,
And liberate the thoughts and deeds of men!
Sound, trump of God! Voice of a thousand years, 1140
Call of the Christ—His clear familiar tone,
Heard in the ages and the aeons past,
Told to the times and worlds that went before;
Call of the Spirit, answered by the blood,
Voice of the Shepherd, by the sheep well known.

    A living prophet unto dying time,
Heralding the Dispensation of the End,
When Christ once more His vineyard comes to prune,
When potent weak confound the puny strong,
Threshing the nations by the Spirit's power, 1150
Rending the kingdoms with a word of flame;
That here the Father's work may crown the Son's,
And earth be joined a holy bride to heaven,
A queen 'mid queens, crowned, throned, and glorified.

    Wherefore came down this angel of the dawn,
In strength divine, a stirring role to play
In time's tense tragedy, whose acts are seven.
His part to fell the false, replant the true,
To clear away the wreckage of the past,
The ashes of its dead and dying creeds, 1160
And kindle newly on earth's ancient shrine

The Light that points to Life unerringly;
Crowning what has been with what now must be;
A mighty still bespeaking mightier.

—-

   Earth rose from wintry sleep[14], baptized and cleansed,
And on her tranquil brow, that seemed to feel
The holy and confirming hand of Heaven,
The warm light in a wealth of comfort streamed;
Nature's great floor green-carpeting anew
For some glad change, some joyful happening, 1170
Told in the countless caroling of birds,
Gilding the foliage, glorying the flowers,
Mirroring mingled hues of earth and sky.

   Glad happening, in sooth, for ne'er before,
Since burst the heavens when Judah's star-lit hills
Heard angel choristers peal joy's refrain
Above the mangered Babe of Bethlehem,
Had earth such scene beheld, as now within
The bosom of a sylvan solitude,
Hard by the borders of a humble home, 1180
Upon that fair and fateful morn was played.

   Players, immortal twain and mortal one,
Standing but fourteen steps upon life's stair,
An unlearned boy, thinker of thoughts profound,
Boy and yet man, dreamer of lofty dreams.

   Not solemn, save betimes, when hovered near
Some wingéd inspiration from far worlds,
Some great idea's all-subduing spell—
His heart grew humbler then, his look more grave;
Not melancholy—mirthful, loving life, 1190
And brimming o'er with health and wholesome glee.
A stalwart spirit in a sturdy frame,
Maturing unto future mightiness.

   Bowing to God, yet bending to no creed,
Adoring not a loveless deity,
That saved or damned regardless of desert,
Ne'er reckoning the good or evil done;
Loving and worshipping the God of love,
The gracious God of reason and of right,
Long-suffering and just and merciful, 1200

Meting to every work fit recompense,
Yet giving more, far more, than merit's claim;
Bowing to Him, but not to man-made gods,
And shunning shameful strife where peace should dwell,
He holds aloof from those degenerate sects,
Bewildering Babel of conflicting creeds,
And pondering the apostolic line,
"Let any lacking wisdom, wisdom ask,
And God will freely give, upbraiding none,"
He puts the promise to the utter test. 1210

    What pen can paint the marvel that befell?
What tongue the wondrous miracle portray?
Than theirs, the Vision's own, what voice proclaim
Whose dual presence[15] dimmed the noonday beam,
Communing with him there, as friend with friend,
And giving to that prayer reply of peace?

    Tell how, as Moses on the unknown mount[16],
From whom in rage fled baffled Lucifer,
Who fain had guised him as the Son of God,
To win the worship of that prophet pure— 1220
Tell how with gloom he strove ere glory dawned,
And black despair met bright deliverance.
Tell how in heart of that sweet solitude,
Within the silent grove, sequestered shade,
While spirit hosts unseen spectators stood,
Watching the simple scene's sublimity,
Eternity high converse held with time;
Time, parent of the hovering centuries,
Mother of dispensations, travailing,
And bringing forth her last and mightiest child; 1230
Heaven's awful Sire, through Him both Sire and Son,
There blazoning the beginning of the end.

    Wane the swift years; the boy a youth now grown;
And on his brow, woe-carved, a world of care.
Bending, an Atlas,[17] 'neath the titan's load,
Daily he climbs the hill of sacrifice,
Viewing from far the mount of martyrdom.

    Nor marvel at his lot; hath he not told—
A crime man ne'er forgave in fellowman—
Told the wise world that God hath spoke again? 1240

"'Twas from below!" Thus bigotry in rage.
"Nay, from above," the meek though firm reply.
"No vision is there now—the time is past."
"But I have seen," affirms truth's constancy.
"God is a mystery, unknowable."
"God is a man—I saw Him, talked with Him."
"Man?" "Ay, of holiness—Exalted Man[18]."

 A strife of words, of warring tongues, now waged,
And weapons vied with words the truth to slay;
Nor truth alone, but her brave oracle, 1250
A boy, by men, by neighborhoods, oppressed.

 Still through his soul the solemn warning rang,
Still from his mouth the startling message flamed:
"No church the Christ's. None, therefore, can I join.
All sects and creeds have wandered from the way.
Priestcraft in lieu of Priesthood sits enthroned.
Dead forms deny the power of godliness.
Men worship with their lips, their hearts afar.
None serve acceptably in sight of heaven.
Wherefore a work of wonder shall be wrought, 1260
And perish all the wisdom of the wise[19]."

 The wrangling sects forgave—well nigh forgot
Their former feuds and fears and jealousies;
And, joining hands, as Pilate Herod joined,
One guilty day when God stood man-condemned,
In friendly reconcilement's cordial clasp,
They doomed to death and hell "this heresy."
None sought, from "Satan's wile," a soul's reclaim,
But all were bent his humble name to blast;
And pious, would-be murder led the van 1270
Of common hatred and hostility.

 But Truth, thou mother of the living thought,
The deathless word, the everduring deed!
What puny hand thy giant arm can stay?
When crushed or backward held, thine hour beyond?
Can bigot frown or tyrant fetter quell
Thy high revolt, O Light Omnipotent!
When God would speak with man, who tells Him nay?
Can hell prevent when heaven on earth would smile?

 Pillowed in prayerful thought the wakeful seer. 1280
Without, broods darkness o'er a dreaming world;

Within, an angel's face turns night to day:
"A messenger from God[20] to thee I come;
Thy sins are pardoned through thy penitence;
Henceforward heard in every creed and clime
The good and evil tongues that trump thy fame.
Behold!"

    Amazement now fresh wonder views;
And while enwrapt, as wave-like visions roll
Their spirit splendors on that gifted gaze, 1290
In words akin to these the tale tells on:

"A slumbering secret hides in yonder hill,
Graven on gold, in characters unknown—
Unknown to thee, but known to me and mine,
The language of my people, ages gone.
Beside the sacred volume, buried there
At His behest who gave my sire command,
The seer-stones, Urim, Thummim, named of old,
Whereby thou shalt dispel the mystery
That hangs above this heaven-favored land, 1300
And Joseph, speaking from the dust, shall join
With Judah, page to page[21], God's grace to tell.

"But be aware, lest Mammon's charm allure,
And tempt from truer wealth that shines within.
More than the lamp the light—be this thy quest:
Seek thou the gold that gilds eternity.

"The winter of the Gentile reign is o'er,
And Israel's springtime putteth forth its leaves.
Fruit planted in the gardens of the past
Hath ripened and is ready for the fall[22]. 1310

"Elias comes[23], Messiah's Messenger,
God's host to summon, and His house to save—
First by persuasion's pleading; that contemned,
By voice of wrath and stroke of violence.
He speaks—the mountains kneel, the valleys rise;
Rolls to the north the land-dividing wave;
Equality—nay, justice, holds the helm,
Each hath his own, the lost lamb finds the fold.
Elias comes—'tis restitution's reign,
And order hurls disorder from the throne. 1320

"War sheathes his fangs, aloft on fearless wing
Peace broods above a restful universe;
A common faith and interest unite,
But conscience still her fullest freedom[24] sees.
Wider than Church extends the Kingdom's bound:
The law from Zion, and the royal word,
The Monarch's edict, from Jerusalem;
A centralized diffusion's balanced sway,
God's might, man's right, in equilibrium.

"Babel no more—stilled all her strifeful tongues; 1330
The primal language[25] o'er the world prevails;
And all is found again as at the first,
While ransomed hosts, rejoicing, shout and sing:
The Lord His ancient people hath redeemed;
The Lord hath gathered all things into one;
And earth becomes a heaven, for she is clothed
In garments as the glory of His light
Who reigneth in the midst, Life's Majesty.

"But ere it break, that bright millennial day,
There falls a nightlier hour than night hath known, 1340
When sun shall frown, moon blush, when dizzy stars,
Drunken with fumes of man's iniquity,
Shall hurl them headlong from their sparkling thrones,
And grovel darkly in the deep abyss;
While heaven shall tremble as if palsy-struck,
Earth as an aspen shaken in the wind.
Men's hearts shall fail, and where be safety found?
For tribulations till that hour unknown,
Save in the feeble typings of the past,
Terrors of famine, fire, and pestilence, 1350
Terrors of whirling wind and whelming wave,
Allied to horrors strange as manifold,
Shall stalk abroad to humble humankind,
To lift the lowly and abase the proud,
To straight the crooked and make smooth the crude,
Jehovah's awful pathway to prepare—
Jehovah, He who cometh to his own,
And by His own at last is recognized.

"No more a lowly Lamb, to slaughter led;
A Lion in his risen majesty— 1360
Lion and Lamb, for gentleness and might,
Mercy and justice, there go hand in hand.

"But first, the sickle in the ripened grain,
Reaping where faith is found, while hope endures,
Drawing the Gentile unto Israel's God,
And gathering the strewn of Abraham.

"Wells truth from earth, pours righteousness from heaven,
Till wisdom's waters inundate the world.
Bestirred the wave by angel trumpets blown,
Wafting the chosen seed to safety's strand, 1370
Winning the West ere yet the East be spoiled.

"Elijah comes—Elijah, he whose rays
Bespeak the Lord of Glory, from whose light
All splendors, paling, hide their tapers dim.
He comes the world to reap, the vineyard prune,
The wheat to garner, and the tares to burn;
He comes, his face a furnace, melting pride,
Consuming wickedness and cleansing worth.
He comes the hearts of sons and sires to turn,
To plant anew the promises of old, 1380
Binding the present to the parent past,
Part unto whole, time to eternity.
He comes the priestly fulness to unfold,
The capstone of life's temple here to lay.
He comes lest man be taken unaware,
And laggard earth be smitten with a curse.

"Hark to that prophet—outstretched Arm of God,
Who comes the ancient order to restore;
And list to him who leads, as Moses led,
The gathered house and host of Abraham!" 1390

Thrice through the night the radiant messenger
In burning words breathed forth the marvel told;
Till memory's page, as traced with pen of fire,
Glowed with each utterance ineffable.

And on the morrow stood the sacred twain—
Mortal, immortal, present linked with past—
Above the spot where slumbering truth reposed;
Not to be wakened yet till autumns four
Had rained their dews upon its resting-place.

Meanwhile the unschooled prophet, angel-taught, 1400
In prayer and patience disciplined his soul;
And visiting yearly that revealing mount,

Learned from its lips a story of the past,
Affirmed in full when risen truth revealed
The pent-up secret of the centuries.

   Words of the angel, Ramah's sentinel,
Custodian of Cumorah's[26] archive old:

CANTO SIX

From Out The Dust[1]

    Jehovah's land—thy country—once mine own,
A sacred soil, a consecrated shore,
Where cometh up the universal Throne, 1410
Dominion that endureth evermore.
Whose God, with gods, in solemn council swore
No tyrant should this chosen land defile;
And nations here, that for a season bore
The palm of power, must righteous be[2] the while,
Or ruin's avalanche ruin on ruin pile.

    Though not till brimmed with guilt their cup of crime,
Ripened the harvest of iniquity.
To races, nations, men, there is a time
To come and go, as wisdom shall decree,— 1420
Wisdom supreme, Tongue of Eternity.
But strikes the hour as men and nations will.
Unfettered in their choice of destiny,
They, by their deeds, the fateful measure fill;
Electing to be clean, or unclean lingering still.

    Race upon race has perished in its pride;
And nations lustrous as the lights of heaven
Have sinned and sunk in reckless suicide,
Upon this ground, since that dread word was given.
Realms battle-rent, and regions tempest-riven; 1430
The wrath-swept land for ages desolate;
A wretched remnant blasted, curst, and driven
Before the furies of revengeful fate;
Till wonder asks in vain, What of their former state[3]?

    Wouldst know the cause, the upas-tree that bore
The blight of desolation? 'Tis a theme
To melt earth's heart, and move all heaven to pour
With sorrow's heaving flood; as when supreme
O'er fallen Lucifer, the generous stream
Of grief half quenched the joy of victory. 1440
Mark how the annals of the ages teem
With repetition. Time, eternity,
The same have taught; but few, alas! the moral see.

There is a sin called self, which binds the world
In fetters fell, than all save truth more strong;
A sin most serpentine, round all men curled,
And in its fatal fold earth writhes full long;
Crime's great first cause, the primal root of wrong,
Parent of pride, and tree of tyranny.
To lay the axe doth unto thee belong. 1450
Strike, that the world may know of liberty,
And Zion's land indeed a land of Zion be!

A choice land, blest above all other lands,
Since earth, reborn, rose sinless from the flood;
Beloved by Him whose holy feet and hands
Were pierced to pour the all-redeeming blood.
Here stands the ancient Altar[4], and here stood
The Ark, till borne triumphant o'er the wave—
The hungry wave that made all flesh its food,
All save a few, whom godly living gave 1460
To see life's single way and shun death's dual grave[5].

The Old World, not the New, by man misnamed;
Cradle and grave of mouldering nations vast;
Whose stalwart spirit stature, seen, had shamed
The mightiest of known empires, present, past.
The land where Adam dwelt[6], where Eden cast
From flaming gate the heaven-appointed pair,
Who fell that man might be; a fall still chaste[7],
Albeit they sinned, descending death's dread stair,
To fling life's ladder down, Love's work[8] and way prepare. 1470

Here rose the Zion of primeval days[9],
Type of a greater Zion yet to rise;
Here Enoch's walls and towers reflung the rays,
Rolled back the flooding splendors of the skies,
Whose portal wide gave welcome. Upward flies
The sainted city, self denied, dethroned:
In all things one, their power e'en death defies:
In dust they ne'er shall slumber; cleansed, condoned,
They wait the final change[10], through Him who hath atoned.

Here cometh up the New Jerusalem[11]; 1480
Here cometh down that risen realm of old,
Jehovah's seat, earth's jeweled diadem,
Joy of the world, by prophet tongues extolled.
Japheth, here joined with Shem[12], finds Israel's fold,

An ark of peace[13] amid a world of war.
The ensign[14] on the mountains here behold!
'Tis Joseph signals Jacob[15] from afar,
And points him to the goal where God and glory are.

    Ancient of Days[16] here sits, as at the first,
When time and earth and Adam's race were young; 1490
When, bowed with age, a great soul's sunset burst
In blessings on his seed. Prophetic tongue,
Thy patriarchal tone through time hath rung!
Michael, the prince, the monarch of our race,
Sire of a world from dust and spirit sprung;
Here sits he, throned in fire; before his face
Ten thousand times ten thousand throng the judgment place.

    Wherefore this land must unpolluted be;
Or, if defiled, by blood again made clean
From grime of sin, from grind of tyranny; 1500
Free from the ills that other lands have seen,
Free from the blots that now dim freedom's sheen.
No nation by vain boasting shall abide;
Bid thine beware, lest here the sanguine scene
Reacted be, and ruin, spawn of pride,
Spring from the soil where nations great as thine have died.

    Hesperia[17], be just—the right maintain,
And foe without, nor foe within, prevails!
Here nations slay themselves, if they be slain,—
Brother 'gainst brother, sire 'gainst son, till fails 1510
The fount of widow's tears and orphan's wails.
Hear thou that servant[18] whom the Father sends—
Hear him and heed, ere Japheth's planet pales,
That peace and freedom may remain thy friends,
While hither, from all lands, all worlds, God's legion[19] wends.

    A gathering from all glories thou shalt see,
Blest land of Joseph[20], honored, lifted high!
Thy brother lands come bending unto thee,
And Gog and Magog[21] menace but to die.
While they that serve the Lord with single eye 1520
Shall see Him in the midst; the goal then won,
When time no longer flecks eternity,
Nor need is there of star, or moon, or sun,
Since He, light's self, is risen, and heaven and earth are one.

    Thus far the angel, Ramah's sentinel,
His vigil keeping on that lonely hill;
And thus the spelled yet speechful auditor,
Around the hearthside of that humble home.
There sire and matron, trusted kith and kin,
Give faithful credence to the story strange, 1530
Pondering the tidings wise and wonderful.

    Thence oft above that mount of mystery,
Of buried lore the solemn sepulchre,
Meet modern seer and ancient oracle.
And while humility at wisdom's feet
Expectant waits, where truth from earth shall spring,
Comes, as from riven tomb, this wondrous tale:

    Where Joseph[22], where wast thou, that time when torn
Was earth asunder; ocean's cleaving sword
The wedded lands wide severing[23]? Where, when borne 1540
Deep through the watery world, as there devoured
By wind and wave that harmless o'er them roared,
The pilgrim sons of Shinar[24]—favored band,
From that far clime where Babel's folly towered
And language foundered on confusion's strand—
Won here a precious heritage, a promised land?

    Preserver of the pure and primal tongue[25],
Most faithful found 'mid living sons of men,
Their leader looked on God; then wrestling wrung
By spirit might, and paged with fiery pen, 1550
The full of what would be, of what had been;
Sealing the secret till an hour should chime
When faith as mighty unto mortal ken
Would bring the marvel of a book sublime[26],
Bridging with lightful lore the shadowy gulf of time.

    But pilgrim prows now part the unknown wave;
Above, around, baptismal billows[27] roll.
Divinity, their guide, protection gave,
Else had engulfing seas entombed the whole.
Though tight each launch, where lines of lustre stole 1560
From molten stones, late struck from Shelem's height[28],
And lit by touch divine. Unto the goal
Of that grim voyage, banishing the night,
Those crystal miracles gave forth their friendly light.

    Till loomed to wistful eyes this waiting land,
Spreading with wing-like continents[29] afar,
As if to welcome worlds. The Chaldean band
The Northland chose, lured by a favoring star,
For South, as North, of human soul was bare.
But liberty loves most a northern zone, 1570
Where nature's ramparts e'en 'gainst nature's war
Put forth protection. Liberty alone
Mahonri's realm[30] might rule—no king, no crown, no throne.

    Still, mighty spirit, thou art manifest!
What creed or clan shall win Columbia's crown?
Though freedom weep, by anarchy opprest,
Hesperia's face reflect Europa's frown,
Sceptered religion ne'er shall tread men down.
Belief and unbelief here find one plane,
That freedom's greater cause[31] be not o'erthrown, 1580
But spring and spread till every tongue maintain
The kingdom of the King whose throne all worlds sustain.

    Here dawns that universal liberty—
Theme of the prophet tongue, the poet pen—
When, winged with power and crowned with purity,
Earth shall be heaven, and gods shall dwell with men;
Fraternity divine, that e'er hath been,
And e'er shall be, the blissful lot of those
Who, conquering self, bind Satan, fetter sin,
And soar beyond the reach of mortal woes, 1590
Rising to sainted heights, as all past Zions rose[32].

    Till then no king upon this crownless land,
Reserved to freedom and to righteousness.
'Gainst her none prosper, lifting hostile hand.
Blest haven, fortressed by God's mightiness[33]!
Kingcraft and priestcraft plant their sure distress.
The past hath spoken—heed the warning tone:
Of pride beware, and baser sordidness—
Self's groveling tyranny, with heart of stone,
Whereby, in ages gone, this land did grieve and groan. 1600

    "Give us a king[34]!" their cry, when power had come,
When wealth was massed, and men were multiplied;
"A king! A king!"—vibrant the echoing dome
From northern lake to gulf and ocean tide;
For Satan in their hearts had planted pride.

Grieved was the nation's wise and watchful sire;
Grieved was the faithful kinsman at his side;
From eyes of both shot gleams of righteous ire,
As voiced ambitious will its ominous desire.

    They sighed: "This leadeth to captivity— 1610
Perchance destruction, ending dark and dire.
Yet must we yield to human liberty
Its own, e'en though a brand from freedom's fire
Kindle for freedom's self the fatal pyre."
So saying, they anointed one their king
Who craved the crown, by patriot son and sire
Put by in pure denial, lest it bring
First care, then crime, and waken woes then slumbering.

    For though a king see duty's pathway plain,
And walk therein, as he who now arose; 1620
What monarch from misrule can all refrain,
When privilege lifts power o'er friends and foes?
Bare is the reign untarnished to the close,
And rarer still the blameless dynasty.
Ofttimes as princes the unkingliest pose,
Because, forsooth, they come of some tall tree,
Whose root and trunk were sound, while branches blasted be.

    True kingliness—what else proves man a king?
A slave, though throned and sceptered, bides a slave;
Nor pride, nor pelf, nor all that power may bring, 1630
Can make the serf a sovereign, or yet save
The dust of either from the common grave.
Royal the soul must be, or comes to end
All royalty. Spirit, then blood, God gave;
And each at last its separate way doth wend
Home to the parent source, to meet no more, nor blend.

    Scarce gone the goodly ruler when his realm
Saw fierce rebellion rear its horrent head.
Usurping treason seized the civic helm,
Wrong trampled right, and justice, judgment, fled. 1640
Ages looked on while battling kingdoms bled.
Lifted the warning voice—its pleading vain:
A blood-drowned continent, a sea of dead,
And, of a mighty people, fallen, self-slain,
A prophet and a king, a solitary twain[35].

That prophet saw the coming of the Lord
Unto the Old, the New, Jerusalem;
Saw Israel returning at His word
From wheresoe'er His will had scattered them;
The realm's wide ruin saw, and strove to stem. 1650
That king, sole scion of a perished race,
Casting his blood-stained sword and diadem,
Lived but to see another nation[36] place
Firm foot upon the soil, then vanished from its face.

Wondrous, indeed, that ancient word and wise;
But wiser and more wondrous still the tale—
The after tale[37] of silent centuries,
Tongued by the guardian of the tome of gold:

Again, athwart the wilderness of waves
Surging old East and older West between, 1660
Where the lone sea a flowery southland laves,
And Zarahemla reigns as ocean queen,
Braving the swell, a storm-tossed bark is seen.
From doomed Jerusalem, to Jacob dear,
Albeit a leper[38], groping, blind, unclean,
Goes forth Manasseh's prophet pioneer[39],
Predestined to unveil the hidden hemisphere.

His lot to reap and plant on this rare shore
The promise of his fathers: Joseph's bough[40],
From Jacob's well, the billowy wall runs o'er; 1670
Abides in strength the archer-stricken bow,
Unto the utmost bound prevailing now,
Of Hesper's heaven-upholding hills. Bend, sheaves
Of Israel, as branches bend with snow,
Unto his sheaf grown mightiest! Here, as leaves
For multitude, the son the great sire's glory weaves.

Ere chimes for him the earth-departing hour,
Summoning a weary soul to restful toil
In risen worlds, where life puts on all power,
Lehi his house convenes,—their hearts the while 1680
Aglow beneath the burning words that pile
A pyramid of prophecy whose spire
Empierces heaven,—and lest they soil
The prospect pure, and tempt Jehovah's ire,
Warns them 'gainst ways of pride and paths of dark desire.

He speaks of Joseph's, Judah's, destiny;
Of blighting and of blessings yet to pour;
Proclaims deliverance his own shall see,
When cometh one the wandering to restore;
Forenames a chosen seer[41] (revealed of yore, 1690
When the boy dreamer's star o'er Egypt rose),
Bringing from dust a blest land's buried lore[42].
Seals then his benison, and eyelids close
To wake on worlds divine, whither, past all, he goes.

The favored son[43] of that prophetic sire—
Favored because most faithful and most just—
Hath soared to sacred mysteries still higher,
And tongued to envious ears the heavenly trust.
And serpent self, that demon of the dust,
Hath coiled and clung around rebellious souls, 1700
Ne'er friendly though fraternal, whose distrust
And jealousy breed bitterness that rolls
Rivers of wormwood 'twixt two races and their goals.

Now peoples twain the Promised Land divide:
Northland and Southland see their tribes increase,
From Arctic floe to far Antarctic tide;
From where the Eastern waves their thunders cease,
To where the Western waters are at peace.
White and delightsome, they that worship God;
They that deny Him, dark, degenerate, these, 1710
Doomed the stern wild to penetrate and plod—
Transgression's scourge and school, the Chastener's heavy rod[44].

The throneless ruler of the regnant race—
King, but no tyrant—prophet, priest, and seer,
Meets upon sacred summits, face to face
(As when to Moses drew Jehovah near),
The Infinite and Spirit Minister[45],
Meets Him as man meets man, and by His grace
The power is given, with seeric eye to peer,
Time's vista viewing through prophetic glass: 1720
Plain to his gaze revealed, the unborn ages pass.

War, slaughter, conquest; heroes, sages, famed;
Kingdoms, republics, empires, rise and fall;
Till pride unknown, and tyranny unnamed,
Where righteous rule brings blessedness to all.
Then self again, the universal thrall.

The faithful, dead or dwindled to a few,
Crime begets crimes the heavens to appall.
Now arrows of God's anger pierce them through,
And horrors piled on horrors make misery's retinue. 1730

    All this and more the prophet-prince foresaw[46];
Messiah's self—Jehovah—Him beheld,—
The Perfect One, in whom was found no flaw,
Though slander as an ocean round Him swelled.
Life's deathless tree—deathless, though demon-felled;
The crash resounding to this far-off shore,
Whose winnowed remnant welcomed Him, revealed
In risen glory, when had ceased the roar
Of wrecking tempests, flung His radiant face before.

    At Whose rebuke the haughty mountains bowed. 1740
Shorn by the whirlwind, sunk, or swept away,
No more their frown the lowly valleys cowed,
Rising like billows 'mid the wrathful fray,
And dashing 'gainst the skies their dusty spray.
Rocks, boulders, hills, no titan strength could lift,
Hurtle as pebbles in the storm-fiend's play.
Earth opes her jaws, and through the yawning rift
Cities, peoples, vanish; of hope, of life bereft.

    Three hours of tempest, and three days of night;
Thick darkness, thunder-burst, and lightning flash; 1750
Millions engulfed, millions in prostrate plight,
Groveling as slaves that feel or fear the lash,
Mingling their groans and cries with grind and crash
Of crags the cyclone's catapult impels,
Whose shrieking flails the fields and forests thrash!
Wild o'er the land roused ocean's anger swells,
And flame's relentless tongue the final doom[47] foretells.

    Three hours of stormful strife—then all is still,
Save for a voice the universe might hear,
Proclaiming what hath hapt as heaven's high will, 1760
Dispensing pardon and dispelling fear.
Anon a mightier marvel doth appear;
Uprolls the misty curtain of the sky—
The midday sun no more their minister,
Greater hath risen! and glories multiply,
As angels in their gaze earthward and heavenward fly.

He greets them as a shepherd greets his flock;
Shows them His wounded side, His hands, His feet;
Then builds His church upon the stricken Rock,
Where flow life's healing waters, limpid, sweet, 1770
As infant innocence[48], that joys to meet
Its great Original. With holy hand
He ministers, bids death and hell retreat,
And singles twelve from out the sainted band,
To sow with words of life the trembling, tear-worn land.

   He bids them prize the truth from heaven outpoured—
What late His tongue hath told, and all that seers
Of earlier days, who owned Him as their Lord,
Have sounded in a world's unwilling ears;
That truth with truth may blend in after years, 1780
As rivers many to one ocean flow;
That when Messiah in his might appears,
Men all may see Him as he is, and know
The Majesty of Heaven, 'mid nations bending low.

   He greets them as His "other sheep"[49]—a fold
Unknown to Judah, but to Jesus known;
And tells of others still, whose fate untold
Hath been the skeptic's scoff and stumbling stone.
All Israel must hear, and one alone
The shepherd be, to guide and govern all. 1790
Where'er, from torrid belt to icy zone,
They wander, they must heed the warning call,
And flee to Zion's shore ere crumbling Babel fall.

   He numbers them with Joseph, known of old,
Whose flock the wolves shall tear in time to come;
Because a wasteful heir his portion sold,
A prodigal forsook the parent dome,
To riot in the wilderness and roam,
Feeding on husks: yet, turning at the last,
Redeemed from darkness, to the Father's home; 1800
And there, the hour of retribution past,
Forgiven, at His dear feet their weary souls they cast.

   Anon He pictures Japheth's destiny[50]:
The Gentile prospering in the Promised Land,
The guardian of the ark of liberty,
So long as he for human right shall stand,
Nor trample on Jehovah's high command.

But woe to them of flinty heart and face
Who from Him turn, to smite with ruthless hand
The withered remnant of a star-ruled race! 1810
For Laman yet shall spring, a lion to the chase[51].

   Vexing the vexer with a vengeance sore,
Who, false to highest hope of human need,
Shall tyrant turn, and play the part no more
Of nursing parent unto Joseph's seed,
For whom a nation founded was and freed,
That from its hand to his fierce house might flow
The promise of his fathers. God shall plead
With Japheth, till his pride shall melt like snow,
Swept from the mountain side, chased by the sun's red glow[52]. 1820

   His word now builds the New Jerusalem—
(Earth-born, though basking in eternal rays)[53],
Which Japheth, blent with Jacob, joined with Shem,
Shall rear on Joseph's land in modern days.
The Father's work of wonder He portrays:—
A servant, marred[54], though hurt not, and yet healed,
Whom wisdom hearkens to, whom faith obeys;
Arm of the Lord, long lying unrevealed,
Uplifted and made bare, His flock to fold and shield.

   Sounds then a parting note, a plaint of woe, 1830
'Gainst coming ages of iniquity,
Ere purifying floods o'er earth shall flow,
And man from sin and self delivered be.
Then, of the twelve, he sanctifieth three[55],
With power o'er death, and gives them to remain
Till comes He in His glory, Lo! they see
The opening heavens receive Him once again;
And marvels else behold, that mortal tongues must chain.

   Three generations pass in righteousness;
A fourth begins, and still from strand to strand 1840
Peace rules, love reigns, and wealth and wisdom bless
The banded nations, walking hand in hand;
Christ's word supreme above a willing land,
Where rich and poor, common their goods, their gold,
Seeking God's glory, free and equal stand,
Loving each one his neighbor, as of old;
Forebeam of day divine[56], when night's dull mists have rolled.

That restful day shall dawn; but e'en as storm,
Darkness and devastation, judgments dire,
Changed with convulsive throe the land's first form, 1850
Made mountains plains, plains mountains, purged with fire
And flood this soil—as saw my nation's sire,
Ere light and peace looked down from realms above;—
So shall it be[57], and more, when heaven's hot ire,
Besoming a world's iniquity, shall move,
In burning, melting might, the gold, the dross, to prove.

Two centuries of love the land caress;
Buried the ancient feud, and banished vice;
When pride, to breed anew the old distress,
Crawls like a serpent to this paradise: 1860
Again the tempter's wiles the weak entice;
Again the fall, the sorrow and the shame;
Again, while angels weep, do fiends rejoice;
For now divided hearts, with hate aflame,
Belie with wicked deeds their righteous faith and fame.

Farewell to peace and power forever past!
Deepest in crime the once delightsome race,
Which melts as would the avalanche if cast
Into the furnace of the red sun's face[58].
Men vie in deeds that devils would debase; 1870
Southland 'gainst Northland strives with might insane;
Backward, still backward, bends the bloody chase[59];
Crimson the land with carnage; main to main
Surges a sea of slaughter—millions are the slain!

The white dissolves; the swart, the red, remains.
Night clothes the continents, and 'thwart the gloom
No ray descends on shadowed peaks or plains,
From history's sun. Darkness, a living doom,
Mantles mind, soul, making the land one tomb.
Then bursts the dawn—breaks forth the East in light, 1880
Where Japheth, cramped and straitened, cries for room.
Rent mystery's veil, naked, in savage plight,
Now occidental realms greet oriental sight[60]!

First found by him whose faith was mightiest,
And now by one whose patience[61] most excels.
Ere storm-pushed prow hath pierced the wordless West,
A kingly soul, unthroned, uncrowned, compels
The homage of a queen. His mind dispels

The gathered gloom of ages; mutineers
And malcontents his presence calms and quells. 1890
Past threatening reefs of bigotry he steers,
And builds a bridge of life that binds the hemispheres.

    The Gentile comes, as destiny decrees,
To Zion's land[62], for freedom held in store,
And Israel's triumph. Friends of freedom, these,
Like to the pilgrim bands that long before
A refuge found upon this sheltering shore.
But followers of right oft wrong the right;
Oppressed become oppressors[63] in an hour;
And now, as day that pushes back the night, 1900
The strong the weak assail, enslave, and put to flight.

    Nor yet can fate forsake them: Japheth's hand
'Gainst Jacob's wrath-doomed remnant still prevails.
Tyrants oppress him from the motherland[64];
The Lord of Hosts a champion arms and mails,
To quell whose might no human power avails;
Nor grander cause or chieftain e'er came forth.
Him as its sire the new-born nation hails,
And e'en would crown the man of matchless worth[65],
Did heaven vouchsafe such king to shame the kings 1910
    of earth.

    But thou hast heard: No king upon this land
From Japheth's loins. Yet shall there come a King,
And Japheth's host with Jacob's equal stand,
While bending nations to that Monarch bring
Their gold, their glory—friendship's offering.
What though invasion, anarchy, shall strive
To strangle right, to poison freedom's spring?
Naught that conspires 'gainst Zion's weal can thrive.
Jehovah—He shall reign, and righteous rule survive. 1920

    Forerunner thou, and thy forerunners these,
Prophet of Ephraim, Joseph's namesake seer[66]!
More than those ancient bridgers of the seas,
Unveiler of the long hid hemisphere,
Whose mystery lies booked and buried here.
Mass thou the might of Joseph, yet to join
With Judah's might, Messiah's throne to rear;
That on this sacred shore may rise and shine
The City Pure-in-Heart—Kingdom of King divine.

    Woe to the tongue that 'gainst thee shall contend! 1930
Break weapons all that smite this iron rod[67],
Beginning of the burden of the end—
The promised fulness of the word of God;
The voice of ages whispering from the sod.
That voice withstood, remaineth shut and sealed
The mightier things in mystery's abode,
Volume on volume slumbering unrevealed,
While wake these lesser truths till now from man concealed.

    Speak thou to Laman's remnant, and reveal
The great things done, the greater yet to do, 1940
That bring deliverance unto Israel.
To white, to red, to men of every hue,
To all redeemed His mighty merit through,
Teach thou the way—tell how by Grace sublime
The spirit gardens[68] of the endless blue
Are visited, each vineyard in its time,
While glad sabbatic bells ring out their grateful chime.

    Earth's hour is nigh—her blest millennial hour,
And dawn there shall a higher, holier day,
Prepared for by these principles of power, 1950
Divinest laws that loftiest worlds obey,
Where gods and angels honor them alway.
There greatest by humility are known,
There order reigns, and right doth all realms sway;
Like claiming like, and cleaving to its own,
Sovereign and subject sharing the glory of the Throne.

    But earth's proud will must bend to will of heaven,
Or twain can ne'er be one, that one for all;—
By angel love the demon lust be driven,
And man set free from self's ignoble thrall. 1960
Let not the mighty task thy mind appall.
What God hath done shall He not do again?
A day of power shall batter down the wall;
The willing heart shall rend the hampering chain;
And o'er this ransomed world, first Son, then Sire, shall reign.

    Proclaim the Dispensation of the End,
Era pre-destined, pre-ordained of yore,
When all of Christ's, on earth, in heaven, shall blend,
And build the Empire of the Evermore.
Ascendeth One who all things shall restore— 1970

The dead to life, the dew-drop to its source.
Spirit must reign, the carnal rule no more;
And this lest earth, winging the sunward course,
Unmeet for such a change, melt 'neath consuming curse.

    Smite thou that sin of self, which binds the world
In fetters fell, than all save truth more strong;
That sin most serpentine, round all men curled,
Within whose fatal fold earth writhes full long.
To loose the coil doth unto thee belong.
To free the soul from sordid tyranny, 1980
Be sacrifice the burden of thy song.
Ay, sacrifice shall set the prisoner free,
And men this truth shall learn, that light is liberty.

CANTO SEVEN

The Arcana Of The Infinite[1]

Flake upon flake, then slide succeeding slide,
The marvel and the wonder multiplied.

Garnered in one vast mind[2] the glacial store,
The glittering avalanche of heavenly lore,
Whose living streams shall slake the burning thirst
Of time unborn, of nations yet unnurst;
Torrent of truth, river of prophecy,
Rolling through worlds to find fulfillment's sea.

He stands, as Moses on the mystic mount,
Where knowledge pours from wisdom's purest fount;
Stands 'neath the droppings of the crystal eaves,
Stands on the loftiest summit man achieves,
Where light eternal—was, is, and to be—
'Lumines the vistas of immensity,
The ultimates of human destiny.

He walks and talks with God, as friend with friend;
He reads the Book of Time from end to end,
And in the Volume of Eternity
Peruses past and far futurity;
Ranges to realms of wider mystery—
Ne'er-ending hope, ne'er-ending history;
While from all depths that sink, all heights that soar,
Come voices, visions, of the Evermore.
Like unto like, above, beneath, the skies,
Deep calls to deep, and faith to faith replies.

He hears the solemn dispensations[3] chime,
From morn till eve, from birth to death, of time;
He notes the markings of the horologe,
The set times of the great unerring Judge;
Then sees those dispensations as they run
Their 'lotted course, like hours 'twixt sun and sun.
Wave after wave rolls o'er the shining sand,
Wave after wave breaks higher up the strand,
With all of weal or woe the ages send.
As sundered ocean tides that shoreward tend,
Now past and future o'er the present pend,

Till on the narrow isthmus sea meets sea, 2020
And time no longer parts eternity.

    He hears the soundings of the trumpets seven[4],
Whose angels, stooping from the heights of heaven,
Proclaim, in tones to rend the echoing spheres,
The secrets of the Seven Thousand Years;
The secret of a book with seven seals,
That all of mortal mystery reveals;
Man's course, God's chronicle, life's tale told true,
Nor tinged with favor's tint, with hatred's hue;
Earth's week of history, whose sabbath chime 2030
Summons to rest the weary soul of time.

    The Holy Order[5] that for aye hath reigned,
For loyal faith and lofty deeds ordained;
The all-creating, all-controlling chain,
Whereby the Gods perpetuate their reign,
Whereby the higher, bending, lift the lower;
Wielding the sceptre of Almighty Power,
Ruling by right the nations, ill aware
Whence came the thrones that have been, thrones that
    are; 2040
Which sets up one and puts another down,
Their fate proclaimed as fortune's smile or frown;
The power that reigns not save in righteousness,
Persuades in meekness, chastens but to bless;
The might of heaven, the pure and potent chain
Stainless, save mortal links their lustre stain,
And plunged through fire are purified again,
He sees extending through the storms of time,
Anchor and cable of a ship sublime.

    Pilots of life on death's fierce tempest tossed, 2050
Love's legionaries, saviors of the lost;
A sacred army's solemn pride and boast,
The janissaries of the heavenly host;
The jeweled circlet of the Central Gem,
Jehovah's body-guard—the Gibborim.

    The guileless followers of the guiltless Lamb,
Of Israel ere Earth knew Abraham[6];
Sealed in the forehead with the sacred Name,
Bearing the Ark of God, the Sword of Flame[7];
Behold them coming, coming, as they came 2060

Whene'er was kindled here the beacon blaze
By each Elias of the olden days!
Truth, error, shine and shadow[8], alternate,
As oft as mankind proves degenerate.

   But ever, as the day-beam sinks and dies,
The stars reset their lanterns in the skies;
And unto Moses in the wilderness
Comes greater light, succeeded by the less[9].
Till truth the fulness of its ray restores,
And heaven o'er earth the holy unction pours, 2070
By ministers upon each hemisphere,[10]
Sent to proclaim what every soul must hear.

   The promise past, fulfillment now is seen,
The Perfect Church[11], resplendent in the sheen
Of risen Righteousness, whose arm once more
Puts forth in power to rescue and restore.
Gray grows to crimson, crimson melts to gold,
And dawns the day by starry night foretold,
Whose lamps prophetic pale their silvery rays,
Lost in the golden light of Latter Days. 2080
A twofold Church, a dual Bride he sees;
Time's the full reflex of Eternity's.

   Visioned the Dispensation of the End,
Where Zions meet, where dispensations blend,
And time's sad rivers cease their mighty moan
In sobbing requiem o'er his sunken throne,
Till death departs, and joy, from zone to zone,
Welcomes the rightful Heir unto his own.

   Visioned the Council of the Ancient One[12],
Where stars make ready for the rising Sun; 2090
Where Adam yields the mortal world he won,
Unto the Sabbath Lord, till sabbath done,
And Sire receives the Kingdom from the Son.
Ere when, award of fulness is there none;
Though great ones gain the far celestial shore,
Shining and perfect as they shone before.

   'Lumed by the Lamp that giveth endless view,
Discerns he spirits false and spirits true;
Unmasking Satan with the keys of light[13],
That blind may see and deaf may hear aright, 2100

A message marvelous to eyes and ears,
The rhythmic message of the songful spheres.

    "Truth is eternal!"—Thus the solemn voice—
"'Twas not her birth made morning stars rejoice,
Nay, but her mission to a new-born sphere,
Whither, as oft, her shining bark would steer
With spirit crew, kin to the kingly race
Peopling the burning orbs of bourneless space.

    "Truth is eternal, endless as its God,
Author and framer of the changeless code, 2110
Ever-returning, oft-repeating plan,
Redeeming from all worlds the race of man.
Life-saving line, far flung from heaven to earth,
To rescue souls—God's wealth, supremest worth—
Rescue the fallen and the penitent,
Who else must bide in hopeless banishment.
Unending were their mortal prisonment,
Did ne'er truth's sunlight gild the gloomy sod,
Gospel of mercy, gift of the gracious God,
Who gave up life to bridge the dark gulf o'er, 2120
And close its cruel jaws forevermore;
Love, striving with belief and unbelief,
Gleaning life's harvest to the latest sheaf.

    "A God whose glory is intelligence,
A God whose knowledge gives omnipotence,
Who makes, maintains, redeems, and glorifies,
Bending to lift the lowliest to the skies,
By triple lever, by the mystic birth,
By Three in heaven, the typed of three on earth:
Water, that signifies obedience, 2130
Sure test of faith, true sign of penitence;
Spirit whereby the flesh is justified,
And blood, whereby the soul is sanctified;—
Lifting by these, but not by these alone,
By every word from Him upon the Throne,
Spirit 'mid spirits, most intelligent[14],
Wherefore their Sovereign Sire benevolent,
Giver of life and light whereby the rest
Press on and on till all things are possessed.

    "Intelligence, eternal[15], uncreate, 2140
Though God-begotten in the spirit state,

Where all creations see maturity,
Ere launched as souls upon the mortal sea,
To prove their worth, make choice 'twixt wrong and right,
And walk by faith as erst they walked by sight;
As free to sound the gulf as soar the height.

"Man a divinity in embryo,
Who, ere he reign above, must serve below;
His spirit in earth element baptize,
For birth and death are baptism[16] to the wise. 2150
The space that parts the lower from the higher,
Spanned by development of son to Sire,
Of daughter unto Mother's high estate,
Where man and woman are inseparate.

"Time a probation; earth, through time, a school,
Where justice reigns, though oft the unjust rule.
Pain, trouble, toil, preceptors of the soul;
Death, birth, but portals to and from life's goal—
Life's fount, where all as infant spirits sprang,
And sons of God in countless chorus sang, 2160
Unheeding earthly sorrow[17]—parent pang
Of after joy, o'er which their triumph rang.

"The fall, whereby the worlds are put in pawn,
And held in durance till redemption dawn,
A plan divine that changeth part to whole,
Immortal spirit to immortal soul.

"Second estate[18] here interlinked with first,
For godliness where spirit life was nurst,
And Satan's rebel host, heaven's third, were sent
To unentabernacled banishment; 2170
Tempters, beguilers, triers of the true,
Who now reap greater gain, or sadly rue
The loss of all, surrendering to him
Who warreth endlessly 'gainst Elohim,
And, shorn of glory, would all light bedim;
Where many, wrecked, to awful depths go down,
While few return to wear the waiting crown,
Reigning where others serve.

          "Each woe, each bliss,
In after worlds, the yield of life in this; 2180
Here garnered are the fruits from fields of yore,
And sown the harvest of the evermore.

"The called are not the chosen past mischance;
The sanctified to glorified advance,
And stewardship becomes inheritance.
Redemption free, for God hath paid the price;
All else man wins by toil and sacrifice.

"As sun, or moon, or varying star[19], appears
Each heir of glory in those endless spheres:
Sun-like the souls that live celestial laws, 2190
And moon-like they who at terrestrial pause—
Who honor not the Saviour in the flesh,
But after, in the spirit realm, refresh
Their fainting, fettered lives at mercy's fount,
And, far as merit buoys them, upward mount;
Saved, glorified, by faith and penitence,
Made valid, through vicarious ordinance[20],
For all who Him believe, who Him obey,
And own in other worlds His sovereign sway.
Nor lost forever souls unsaved today: 2200
Telestial they who taste the pangs of hell,
And pay guilt's debt ere they in glory dwell,
Twinkling as stars whose numbers none can tell.

"Souls that to high celestial realms have won,
Dwell with the gods, beholding Sire and Son;
While bounds are set that bar terrestrial heirs
(With whom the Gracious One his presence shares),
And dwellers in the far telestial spheres,
To whom the Holy Spirit ministers.
God's servants these, but to His glorious home— 2210
The loftiest heights of heaven—they cannot come.

"Justice and Mercy each shall have its own,
Nor one thrust other from the dual throne;
Each shoal and deep a final fullness see,
And like clasp like through all eternity.

"But who shall sound the bottomless despair
Of one condemned the second death to share?
If, re-ensnared in Satan's subtle mesh,
A soul redeemed its Saviour pierce afresh,
Spurning the Spirit, scorning proffered ruth, 2220
A traitor utterly to light and truth,
Then flames perdition's gulf, death's last abyss,
The lake of fire, all life's antithesis.

All power then powerless to change its plight;
For what avails the burnt-out lamp to light?
Justice can lay no blame on blameless shelves,
Nor mercy save when souls will damn themselves.

 "Twofold is death, but life has threefold sway;
What ne'er created was, endures alway.
The organized disorganized may be, 2230
But not the life that lives undyingly.
Nothing bides nothing: that which is shall be;
Though form, not essence, change unceasingly.
Space, spirit, matter, all eternal are,
And death but on creation wages war.
Whate'er beginning had may have an end,
But life eternal doth itself defend.

 "Man's inmost spark, his being's primal fire,
As birthless and as deathless as its Sire,—
No more the maker of that unmade germ 2240
Than man the framer of the spirit form,
Born and begotten in the first estate,
God's creature, whom God's power can uncreate.
Spirit to spirit, dust to dust returns,
But bright intelligence forever burns,
Though banished from the presence of the light,
Exiled and wandering in the outer night,
Remembering past, and mourning present blight,
The end whereof, a mystery to man,
Unsolved while bending 'neath the mortal ban, 2250
None but the doomed partaker e'er shall scan.

 "Higher than heaven, deeper than hell, profound,
His course wherein no crookedness is found—
An onward, upward, never-ending round.

 "Comes forth all life at resurrection's call,
When soul immortal sheds its mortal thrall;
The just first rising, who with Christ shall reign,
While sinners tarry till He sounds again,
Late issuing, in shame and self contempt,
When Lucifer, unbound, shall newly tempt, 2260
Still striving for a glory not his own,
Till by the Arm Almighty overthrown.

 "Spirit and body, blending, make the soul,
As halves, uniting, form the perfect whole.

Spirit and element, commingled, one,
Inheriting the Glory of the Sun,
Symbol a greater union yet to be,
When heaven and earth shall wed eternally,
And restitution's edict seal and bind
Eternal matter to eternal mind, 2270
Like unto like, for night weds not with day,
And order's mandate e'en the gods obey.

   "The sealing of the sexes, mate to mate,
Earnest of exaltation's lofty state,
Where evermore they reign as queens and kings,
And endless union endless increase brings;
While serve as angels the unwedded ones,
Abandoning their right to royal thrones.

   "One are the human twain, as sheath and sword—
Woman and man, the lady and the lord; 2280
Each pair the Eve and Adam of some world,
Perchance unborn, or into space unhurled.

   "From endless spirit, endless element,
The worlds that glow in glory's firmament.
Created all and governed all by law,
Perfect they shine, or show sin's fatal flaw;
Their Maker's will obey or disobey,
And felons found a felon's debt[21] must pay;
While wiser orbs, obedient at school,
Are robed in radiance, and have learned to rule— 2290
Are lords of light, resplendent and supreme,
E'en as great Kolob 'mid the kokaubeam.

   "Earth a celestial law hath magnified[22],
And by that law shall she be sanctified,
And by the same shall she be glorified;
By fire refined, the gold from dross set free,
Shining forever as a crystal sea,
Celestial seer-stone[23], making manifest
All things below to souls upon her breast—
Chosen, omniscient, children of the Sun, 2300
Offspring of Adam, Michael, Ancient One,
Who comes anon his fiery throne to rear,
His council summoning from far and near.
Ten thousand times ten thousand bow the knee,
And "Father" hail him, "King," eternally.

"For so are governed all those worlds of fire,
That chorus in a universal choir
The glory of the Lord Omnipotent,
Whose power hath framed through infinite extent
The splendors of the flashing firmament; 2310
Sire of the universe, and King of Kings,
O'er countless realms; each dusty dot that springs
To blazing being, empire of a god,
Who equals Him, yet owns His sovereign rod,
The Central Scepter of Omnipotence,
The God of Gods, Supreme Magnificence,
Regnant o'er all that is or e'er shall be,
Throned on the summit of eternity.

"Souls there above who once below all things,
All things inherit, and are priests and kings, 2320
Pillars immovable, princes unto God,
No more outgoing from that high abode,
Where past and future present are alway,
And years a thousand even as a day".

Who here have lived, or would have lived, the law[24],
Exalted, numbered with the gods, he saw,
One with the wisdom of Omniscience,
And glorious with All Intelligence.
So thorough and so just the perfect plan,
Weighing the motive with the work of man! 2330

Nor this the tithe of what those tongues unfold,
Nor tithe of tithe of what can ne'er be told.
As unto Judah's one and Joseph's three[25],
Who tasted of translation's ecstacy;
Or him who, spared from Babel's doom, beheld
Messiah's unclothed spirit[26], faith-compelled;
Or him of Tarsus, tranced, the triple seer[27]
Of things unlawful to be uttered here;—
As unto souls like these was given to see
The marvel past, the mystery to be, 2340
So upon him, their peer of modern days,
The Source of all-revealing sends its rays.

Broken the fountains of the upper deep;
Opened the sepulchres where ages sleep;
The past, the future, now the present leaven;
With truth from earth blends righteousness from heaven,

Welding the parted links of being's chain,
Old making new, the dead live again.

   O message marvelous to eyes and ears!
Voices and visions of the mystic spheres! 2350
Voices of noonday, visions of the night,
Whisperings of angels, and their presence bright!
Voice of the Architect of Life's vast Plan,
Speaking as God to God, as man to man!

CANTO EIGHT

The Lifted Ensign[1]

Armed now with knowledge, panoplied with power,
With two-edged sword of God's authority,
Girded by heavenly hands on shepherds twain[2],
The first and second of a gathering flock,
Transcribers of the buried book of gold,
Whose mystic page, unsealed by gift divine, 2360
Save part withheld of mightier mystery,
Now challenges the wise and wondering world;—
Armed and equipt, with staff, and stone in sling,
Strong in the Lord, the God of Israel,
The dauntless David of a later day
Fares forth to meet the Giant of Untruth[3].

Thenceforth a warrior and a wanderer,
A victor hated for his victories;
Targe for the javelin of jealousy;
Hunted and hounded through the wilderness; 2370
Outlawed by all, all save a loyal few,
The patient sharers of his painful lot,
Companions of his mortal pilgrimage,
Recalled with him, their earthly errand o'er,
To grace the courts of High Jerusalem.

But ere a day for that departure dawns,
Unveiled once more the face of mystery.
Speaks from the musty tomb of buried time,
The all-remembering Spirit of the Past:

"Time yet was young[4], but old iniquity, 2380
Outcast of worlds redeemed, on earth was rife,
And, self-enchained, a fallen race lay prone
At feet of Lucifer. And demons laughed,
And hell rejoiced, and all that ribald host
Clapt hand, and danced and jeered derisively;
While gods and angels wept, their pitying tears
Whitening the spectral mountains cold and lone,
Wakening to virile springs a spirit waste.

"And there the sainted commonweal[5] arose,
Haven divine, hill of the sanctified, 2390
Oasis-like 'mid burning sands of sin;

God's people, pure in heart, and one in all,
No poor among them, pride and greed unknown;
Saved by the tidings first to Adam taught,
And next to Enoch's generation told.

   "Righteous, they dreamt no evil, feared no ill,
And death, the universal doom, defied.
Earth not their pillow; they shall one day pass
From mortal to immortal painlessly.

   "Self's chain was sundered[6]; devils glared aghast, 2400
And gnashed their teeth with disappointed rage,
Trembling in terror lest perdition's pit
Engulf them ere the time. Then gathering power,
As if for Armageddon's conflict[7] dire,
When triumphs Michael o'er the foe unchained,
Hell's molten belch of burning hatred hurled
Upon those hapless sons of earth who scorned
The refuge of the righteous; her bright towers,
Far-beaming with terrestrial radiance[8]—
The promise fair of full celestial change,— 2410
Bidding the vile beware, nor venture near
The awful mountain of God's holiness.

   "Waxed foul the world in wickedness, piled high
A hideous monument of shame and crime,
Which, toppling with its own weight, crashing fell,
Whelming in ruin the guilty race of man,
Whose spirits, as fierce seas their dust devoured,
By fiercer fiends to dungeon deeps were driven.
Nor thence redeemed till He who died for all
Soared from the cross to set the captive free[9]. 2420

   "The while, on fearless wings of purity,
Cleaving as bird or ransomed soul the air,
The sainted city entered into rest,
Envied of Babel, climbing robber-like[10];
Bride of the Highest, midway hovering,
Till folded in the bosom of the Gods,
Where Zions from unnumbered worlds have fled.
Type temporal of spirit antitype,
A future moral height foreshadowing.

   "Foreseen the fatal deluge. Ere the doom 2430
Of all save faithful Noah and his seven,—
Tri-branching tree[11] of race regenerate,

Yielding anew life's fruit and foliage,—
Earth mourned as Rachel, Rizpah, o'er the slain,
The slain of men unborn, who yet must die
Degenerate in the days that were to be.

   "Then Enoch wept, and sued in sympathy,
And God gave answer thus:

            'Earth yet shall rest,
And, sanctified, shall see her Saviour reign, 2440
Monarch of worlds, His realms as ocean sands.
But it shall be within the latter days,
The days of vengeance and of wickedness,
When men the Sole-begotten crucify,
And He shall go again to judge the world,
Proclaimed by truth, forerun by righteousness,
Gathering the pure-in-heart unto a place—
A holy place my people shall prepare,
There to await my coming, mine and thine.
Then shown the resurrection's shadowing: 2450
Zion above, from all creations past,
Shall meet and blend with Zion from below;
Spirits and bodies of the just shall join,
And in the midst my tabernacle be.
Yea, as I live, so will I forth again,
My oath to thee, my covenant, to fulfill;
And earth shall garb in glory of her God,
And Noah's righteous seed in Me rejoice.'"

   These things spake God to Moses, from the mount
Whose name is veiled to ken of humankind; 2460
And thus that prophet, but through unbelief
And cunning craftiness, at war with Light,
The fulness of his message sleeps till now,
When one like unto him[12] and Him he typed,
Brings forth the buried meaning from its grave.

   On twain of ocean-parted hemispheres,
Saw noon of time a twofold type[13] of peace,
A pledge, a token, of millennial rest,
An earnest of the Commonweal to come;
But no fulfillment of the promise old, 2470
No ripe fruition of the ancient oath,
To Enoch sworn, through Moses re-affirmed,
By Ephraim's prophet made to live again.

Promise now sought fulfillment[14],—it was time;
For weary earth lay groaning 'neath her load.
"Unclean, unclean," her cry, as leprous sin
With foul intent clasped close her shrinking form,
And baned with foetid breathing all her soul.

Long she had mourned and wept o'er life's decay;
Her waning strength, from age and weariness, 2480
Her mother powers, unholy passion's prey,
Bringing, in lieu of giants, pygmies forth,
To fall untimely on her withered breast.
Dwindling and dwarfed in all save wickedness,
And knowledge, oft made pander unto ill,
With learning gorged, for wisdom famishing,
Man both a glutton and a starveling seemed.

For Self, the sordid, sat once more enthroned,
Binding in servile chains a universe,
Where mightily men strove for place and fame, 2490
Greedy for power, as gluttonous for gold.
And who sought neighbor's weal, save kith and kin
Or petted friendling prest a favored claim?

Disorder reigned, and satire laughed to scorn
Grotesque, invidious inconsistency:
Talent on title waiting, brain on birth!
Genius at oars, and dullards at the helm!
The prancing war-steed fastened to the plow,
The ass unto the chariot—oft with rein,
Curbing the mettled courser's noble rage, 2500
Or goading him with needless cruelty!

Matter was monarch; Spirit stood apart,
Unknown, unseen, or spurned and thrust aside
By thronging myriads, bending supple knee,
And basking in the proud usurper's smile.

Men bowed not down to sun and moon and stars,
To bird, nor beast, nor reptile, as of yore;
But worshipt still at other creature shrines,
Ignoring the Creator's primal claim.

Pride sneered at poverty—if poor of purse, 2510
But gave its hand to beggared intellect,
To bankrupt soul, and greeted them as peers.

Learning, if lowly pillowing its head,
A pauper deemed, and pitied or condemned.
And many, stung by adder glance of scorn,
Shunning a life of noble toil and care,
To Mammon, e'en in marriage, sold themselves,
Offering a lawless fire at passion's shrine,
Or staining hands and heart with sabler sins.

 Shameful the serfdom of the earth-bound soul, 2520
Base passion's basest slave and prisoner;
Charmed by no music but the clink of coin;
Cankered and crusted o'er with avarice;
Dupe, dreaming shadow real, and substance show.

 Where party more than principle was prized,
Where private gain was labeled "public good,"
And "patriotism" masked hypocrisy,
Science, when sordid, or subservient
To worldly ends, to aims material,
Stood pedestaled and robed in honors rare: 2530
While art fell fainting at the patron's door,
Or starved and froze in cheerless attic den.

 For aye the flesh must first be comforted,
And e'en the body's luxuries abound,
Ere mind of man may clothe its nakedness,
Or hungering heart and spirit have their own.

 Music, the drama, all art, still divine,
Though oft to ends ignoble basely bent,
In atmospheres miasmic, fever-fraught,
To folly pandering and to lechery; 2540
Or using gifts God-lent for good of all,
Gain's maw to glut, fame's lust to gratify.
Forgot the Giver, and adored the gift,
As in the pagan days of olden time.

 And thou, where thou, O sage philosophy,
Heir to a hundred shadows of thy name!
Where thy spent waves on speculation's strand?
Still striving, finite for the infinite,
Man groping for the mystery of God,
A river that would fain engulf the sea! 2550

 Religion dead, and poesy so deemed,
Because unwedded to a carnal age,

Unprostituted to its paltry aims,
Or hid beneath vast verbal rubbish heaps,
The dust and debris of the former fires.
Religion dead, but bigotry alive,
And ne'er more active upon earth than now,
When sect 'gainst sect in battle order stood,
And schisms and dissensions multiplied.
Some worshipt nothing, naming it a god; 2560
Some deemed the mortal dust a thing divine;
Religious, irreligious, bigotry,
Each counted victims by the hecatomb.

    What wonder, when truth's meanings tortured were,
The living God dethroned, and in His stead,
A monster crouching on the Mercy Seat,
Whose mere caprice, naught else, did save or damn?
Wafting the blood-stained criminal to bliss,
If he but gasped, half hung, the holy Name?
Thrusting the spotless infant into hell, 2570
If un-elect, or unbaptized for sin!
To endless woe or weal forefating all.
What wonder justice, reason, stood aghast,
While faith, revolting, rushed to doubt's extreme?

    Critics, high-soaring, sought to clip the wings
Of arrogance in all creeds save their own.
Half-fledged conclusion, findings premature,
Grounded on tale of rock or ruin old,
More credence had, more reverence, from men,
Than sacred lore of heaven-lit centuries. 2580
All miracle was myth, nor aught worth while,
Save, leaded down with learned theories,
It crawled, an earth-worm, wanting will to climb
Above the level of the commonplace.

    Fanatics in the state as in the church,
Their prejudices palmed for principle,
Vain vagaries and dreams for doctrine sound;
And woe to him who lisped of liberty,
Or thought aloud one thought unthought before!
Freedom to think and breathe—God-granted boons, 2590
Alike, to savage, serf, and citizen—
Was all that freedom signified to some,
Who, as they doled a gift already given,
Boasted themselves magnanimous and wise.

Freedom to speak and act as conscience bade,
As God commanded, crushed or captive bound,
E'en where men vaunted most of liberty.

   And peace was yet a dream unrealized,
For war still sowed and reaped his harvests red;
And Christian guns were mightiest and slew most. 2600

   Nor yet stood toil 'gainst capital arrayed,
The starving masses 'gainst the Midases,
As erst arose, 'gainst moss-grown old regimes,
The trampled Terror[15], scrawling with fierce hand
On history's flaming scroll his red revenge,
With that blood-reeking pen, the guillotine;
Nor yet faced frowning mass contemning class[16],
Jeering, oblivious of the lurking doom,
The glooming clouds where groaned the gathering storm.
But murderous craft and oath-bound anarchy, 2610
With secret deeds of darkness, had begun
To sap the life of human government,
And plot against the safety of mankind;
While greeds and lusts and passions manifold,
Preying on frailty and on innocence,
Ran riot 'mid the fairest, brightest, best.

   Where, promise, thy fulfillment, pledged of yore?
'Twas time—full time—the far-seen ensign waved,
Hailing the morn on heights of holiness,
Proclaiming peace and freedom to the world. 2620
'Twas time disorder fled, time justice reigned,
And rightfully were held dominion's keys;
Time pure religion's sceptre should return,
By poesy extolled, by art adorned,
With science and with reason reconciled;
Time feeble earth her panacea found,
Time health gave life its old longevity,
Time pride should bend, time lust to love should yield,
And self confess the joy of sacrifice.
'Twas time an Enoch came[17], a Zion rose. 2630

   Sound, trump of God! as when old Jordan's wave
Shook with the thunder-tread of Joshua's host,
Shook with the shouting and the trumpet blasts,
Heard the loud roar of crumbling Jericho,
And in mad haste ran shuddering to the sea!

Speak now the doom foreshadowed by that fall—
The mightier doom of Modern Babylon:

   Bow down thy head, proud mistress of the world!
Humble thy haughty crest, degenerate queen!
Lift but thine eyes to where God's finger glows 2640
In fiery warning on thy festal wall,
Drowning in dread the voice of revelry,
Thy saturnalia's ribald shout and song.
Ended thine empire, Weighed-and-Wanting-Found!
Down to the dust in all thy worldliness,
Thou thing of brass, of iron, and of clay!
Sound, trumpet, sound! The looked-for signal looms!
The fateful stone upon the image rolls!

   "On you, my fellow servants, I confer
The priestly power of Aaron, with the keys 2650
Of angel ministries, of penitence,
Of water-birth that washes free from sin.
And greater things than these shall yet be given—
The holier powers of high Melchizedek,
Which Mightier by three shall minister."

   And on each head was laid a holy hand[18];
Time making good the promise plighted there,
Welding another link in wonder's chain,
Writing new chapters of a story strange,
Confounding human learning, fools and wise. 2660

   So came once more the panoply of power[19].
So rose the ensign o'er a waiting world.

   Armed thus with knowledge and authority,
Armed and equipt, with staff, and stone in sling,
Fares forth a champion for Israel,
To grapple with Philistia and prevail.

   Guide unto God, repointer of the path,
Untrodden through a thousand years nigh twained,
The while men roamed, as once o'er trackless wild,
The savage, by the untaught trapper trained; 2670
Blind leading blind through thick and thorny wold.

   Light 'mid the darkness, beam from heaven's full blaze,
Driving the mists, that comprehended not

His brightness nor their own obscurity;
Holding him blind who saw as few have seen.
He, blind, forsooth, who more than all beheld!

    Sinking deep shafts to mines of mystery,
Shallow and empty to the worldly wise;
Soaring to heights by human lore undreamt,
Yet deemed an earth-mole, groping, groveling. 2680

    Aloft, alone, an exile among men,
A wanderer in a solitary way,
Pariah of prejudice and unbelief,
Whose lowering features fiercely on him frowned.
Thought's prisoner and truth's, that maketh free
The spirit, though the body pine in chains,
Albeit the tongue, the pen, in durance be,
Consigned to silence, captive unto light,
And crucified betwixt ideal and real.

    But who art thou that lookest forth sublime, 2690
A soul upsoaring as from sepulture,
Body and spirit pure and free from stain,
As gold and silver tried by seven-timed fire?

    Speak! Art not thou the Woman Wonderful[20],
Summoned from out the silent wilderness,
Arisen from the grave of centuries,
No more to be despoiled or trodden down?
A symbol of exalted sanctity,
The consecration of the contrite heart;
Of ancient types the modern complement, 2700
Chief splendor of time's sparkling firmament,
Whose silver stars bespoke this sun of gold.

    But when did darkness comprehend the day?
When welcomed pleasure thorn-crowned sacrifice,
Whose higher, holier joys than sin can know,
As dust and ashes to the sensual soul?
Jewels to swine, that, turning, rent the hand,
And fain 'neath foot had torn and trampled all.
Such was Truth's fate, alas! in modern time,
'Mid Christian men;—but not her final fate. 2710

    For who can stay the sun-like march of Truth?
Who dim with bloody hand her beam divine?
First shall he halt the progress of the stars,

The bright procession of the infinite;
Blot out the day-beam, dull the scythe of time,
Shear morning's wings, roll back eternal night,
Or shake the moveless throne of destiny.

   Lifted an ensign never to be furled,
Unsheathed a falchion evermore to flame,
Till earth-born realms, in one wide empire rolled, 2720
Hail conquering Christ as life and light of all.

CANTO NINE

Upon The Shoulders of The Philistine[1]

The Eaglet's nest is empty[2]—void the lair
Of the young Lion. Where, O Ephraim, where?

Where billows break along a storied strand[3],
Heroic wave, a fair and favored land.
Realm of a rising glory—this thy name!
The cradle of the Kingdom—this thy fame!

There rose the morn—though flecked with fire and blood—
The morn benign of human brotherhood,
Foredestined to a passing cloud's eclipse. 2730

Self-trammeled cause, harried by hounds and whips
Of persecution, whose infuriate maw,
Usurping oft the form and force of law,—
To lawless hands a far too ready rod,—
Had fain engulfed the growing work of God.

Widowed, bereft, a land left desolate,
A wounded bird that mourns a driven mate,
The plumage from its bleeding body torn,
And scattered wide o'er realms remote, forlorn.

On, Ephraim, on! thy pilgrim flight renew. 2740
Land of the Sun—Shinea's land[4]—adieu!

Yet stay! Ere storm could burst, was visioned there,
Within the portal of the House of Prayer,
A promise, a fulfillment, long foretold:
Elias and Messias there behold!
With angel keepers of the ancient keys
Of gathering and of sealing mysteries.
Haloed with fire, while burns the heavenly glow,
Upon the Prophet they their powers bestow[5].

Speed then swift messengers his face before, 2750
To blaze his sacred name on every shore;
Chosen and missioned from the sending skies,
The slumbering nations to evangelize.
Resounds 'gainst error's shield truth's ringing lance,
Unlettered light 'gainst learned ignorance;
Priestcraft dethroned, by Priesthood downward hurled,
While ancient thunder shakes the modern world.

Already, to redeem red Laman's bands[6],
Have virile footprints prest those virgin lands,
Where westering empire, in creative might, 2760
Rolls a new world upon the wondering sight;
Where flower-starred prairies, in the far extent,
Kiss with soft lips the bending firmament,
And sea-like rivers, solitary, lone,
Pour their proud waters toward the burning zone.

Land of all lands the rarest[7], where shall rise,—
Mirrored magnificence of earth and skies,
Each gate a pearl, each pinnacle a gem,—
The jasper walls of New Jerusalem;
The golden glory of the hemispheres, 2770
Jehovah's throne through all the Thousand Years.
The land where Adam fell, where Enoch rose,
Where time began and history shall close.

Thereto and thence, by brand and fagot driven,
His fault to man, his fealty to heaven,
With here and there, perchance, an idle word
Vainglorious zeal or vengeful might afford,
Flies Ephraim, scorched and scourged, from Japheth's
   wrath[8],
Pushed on and on o'er steep and thorny path, 2780
Whipt, plundered, wounded, bleeding, to the goal,
Where joy in fullness crowns the conquering soul.

Then hath not war, that bringeth woe and pain,
The right betimes, like gentle peace, to reign?
What strife, what tempest, wreaks its wrath in vain?
Prosperity and persecution blend,
As sun and storm, faith's branch with fruit to bend.
Twain are the shoulders[9] of the Philistine,
That Israel onward bear, as breeze and brine
The tempest-driven bark that safe o'er sea 2790
Carried calm Caesar[10] and his destiny.
Progression fails with opposition's flight,
And darkness is but handmaid unto light.

Mistrustful of "the law of liberty[11],"
Sounding from far the doom of slavery,
Maddened by jealous fear, the Gentile sees
Peril in purling stream, in whispering breeze,
Telling of wondrous thrift, of mystic power,

Of spirit gifts—the Bride's becoming dower;
Sees menace[12] in that migrant fold's increase, 2800
A menace to his power, his pride, his peace;
And, as of old, when Egypt's despot frowned
On Jacob's increase, growth from fruitful ground,
Or when fell Herod, fain to slay life's Lord,
Pierced Rachel's bosom with unpitying sword;
With feigned or real suspicion of intent
That could but lurk in minds by malice bent,
And ne'er found lodgment in the dreams of those
Now fearfully beset by whelming foes,
Force joins with fraud, impelled by lust of crime, 2810
And innocence bewails the evil time.

   A second Pharaoh now o'er Israel see!
A Herod[13] in the home of Liberty!
Where wingĕd Nemesis shall find her own,
Gathering the whirlwind[14] where the wind was sown.

   Friendless, unsheltered, forth the exiles go,
Lit by their burning homes athwart the snow,
Till crimson footprints stamp the frozen path,
And icy billows bar them from the wrath
Of cruel fiends, whose fellows, masked as men, 2820
Where languish sons of light in darksome den,
Gloat, while they guard, and flout with jest obscene
The helpless victims of that heartless scene;
Exulting foully, boastingly, the while,
O'er deeds none else than devils would defile.

   Till patience, past enduring, dures no more;
Heard, above jackal's yell, the lion's roar.
Thunders and flames Jehovah's threatening rod,
And shakes the dungeon[15] with the wrath of God—
A lightning tongue to scorch His cowering foes, 2830
And scourge them to the kennels whence they rose.
When known such power, such might of word and will,
Since Christ bade tempest sleep and waves be still?

   Free, whereso'er he wends, is hope renewed,
Demons unhoused, disease and death subdued[16].

   Where Sire of Waters[17] sweeps o'er silvery sands,
Prest by the pilgrim feet of many lands,
Aloft, alone, a sacred city stands.
City, mother of many[18], none more rare,

A blossoming waste shall yield, now burnt and bare; 2840
City, mother of empire, famed as fair,
Whose birth the solemn muse must yet declare.

    Where groaned the land with dread malarial ill,
Healed by a hand divine, o'er vale and hill
See roof and dome and glittering fane arise!
Unworldly link[19], rewelding Earth and Skies!

    Then comes Elijah's mightier mission[20] forth,
And mortal vows take on immortal worth,
Kindling anew hope's ever living fires,
Turning the mutual hearts of sons and sires, 2850
While doors to spirit dungeons open swing,
That love to light the living dead may bring!

    But gaze from sinking unto soaring sun!
Beyond the wave the conquering word hath won
Past horrent hosts of Lucifer that rose,
With wrath of man, the message to oppose.
Vain strife, where fiends archangels would assail,
Warring 'gainst mightiness that must prevail—
Prevail to save a periled ship. 'Tis done;
The crisis past[21] with Albia stormed and won; 2860
East floweth West—"The Gathering" hath begun.

    And now, to fruitful lands, 'neath favoring skies,
Befriended by the just[22], the brave, the wise,
Till truth, too mighty for the common ken,
Hath put a sword betwixt the souls of men,
Fares garnered Ephraim, earliest offering[23]
Of Israel's hope, Idumea's harvesting.

    Nations besprent with Abrahamic blood
Meet there and mingle in that widening flood.
Impelled by helping hand or hostile power, 2870
By friendly looks or frowns that darkly lower,
Gathers the flock of faith from every land
Where roving Ephraim mixt with Japheth's band;
Philistia's shoulder bearing Israel's flight,
That Japheth, too, may come to Zion's light,
And Joseph be o'er all his brethren blest,
A saviour in his Egypt of the West[24],
Where corn and wine, 'mid famine, comfort life,
Where peace and plenty shame a world at strife,
And, bending from the ice-barred North, shall come— 2880

As bent their stars in his, the dreamer's dome—
Assyria's long lost captives[25], wending home.

    Westward, far westward, chase the lingering night,
Impelling Spirit! Angel of the Light!
Westward, still westward, till the morn shall burn
In high meridian glory; till shall turn
Fate's restless tide, re-rolling o'er the East,
Spoiling the spoiler, spreading freedom's feast,
Foiling dark anarchy, thy fellest foe,
Land, chosen land! stunned, staggering 'neath its blow; 2890
Rallying the loyal[26] in a common cause,
Rending the eagle from the bear's red claws;
Hurling invasion backward o'er the Isles,
Building anew upon the olden piles,
Beginnings of the crowning commonhood—
A modern Zion where the ancient stood.

    Backward, roll backward, river of the blood!
Back to thy fountain, hurrying human flood—
To Adam's land, the far Edenic shore;
For last is first and old is new once more, 2900
And nations rise where nations fell before!

    Joseph, uprisen from the grave-like mound,
His ancient and inglorious battle ground[27],
Retreads with modern step the painful path
Where erst he fled[28], a fugitive from wrath;
Fated to flee till ebbs that westward flow,
Bearing from Japheth bitter curse and blow,
While patient heaven holds off the woeful fate
That cometh swift and layeth desolate
The powers that prey on Jacob—all that hate 2910
The God of Joseph, and the just decree
That builds him here a boundless destiny.

    Westward, burn westward, morn divinely bright!
Morn of Jehovah, morn of Jacob's might!
But stand thou still on Zion, glorious light!
For there must dawn the day that knows no night.

    Beginnings that have here in beauty stood,
Prone, as from withering fire or wasting flood,
A little season wrecked and ruined lie[29],
Till they that build put pride and passion by, 2920

And, taught by pain, through suffering's fiercest fires,
Part with all lustful, covetous desires.

    When faith shall wear the armor without flaw,
And union such as sainted Enoch saw[30]
Honors the fullness of celestial law,
Then—sword of God and blade of Gideon,
Dazzling, confounding, driving on and on,
Till besomed as with fire the fated land,
Where Zion, guileless, glorious, shall stand,
A terror only to her trembling foes[31], 2930
Ensign of peace and Eden of repose,
Where life's tree blossoms and light's fountain flows.

    Meanwhile her valiant ones, her tried and true
Daughters and sons, shall they not dare and do?
In vain, alas! in vain of such to sing,
With trembling hand a tuneless harp I string.
For who can count the cost, the painful price,
Measure the sorrow and the sacrifice,
Rare spirits of a more than Spartan race
Compelled their souls of halting dread to face? 2940
Harp of the Hebrew seer! Be thine to break
The muse's slumber, bid the world awake,
And glow o'er deeds yet done for conscience' sake.
What tongue than Zion's own can loose the spell?
Whose voice than modern Leah's, Rachel's, tell
The story of a burden borne so well?

    Bending, not breaking, 'neath thy load of care,
Sowing to joy, thou shalt not reap despair!
Planting the hope of human purity,
That righteousness may crown futurity,— 2950
Patience! endure! for pain shall bring thee power[32].
Time but a dream—eternity thy dower.
Where perfect love casts forth the jealous fear,
A diamond in thy diadem each tear;
And every sigh that rent thy suffering breast,
A wave of rapture on the shores of rest.
My lot as thine, purest of pure-in-heart!
Be mine the bitter as the better part.

    But sorrows else have shadowed all things there;
The voice of mourning drowns the voice of prayer. 2960

Dampened e'en now with death's prophetic dew,
Thy cold, pale brow, O fated, fair Nauvoo!

   Remains for thee no peace, for thine no rest,
Till on the parching plain, the frozen crest;
A desert land of unlocked mystery,
Frowning on hope, and dumb to history.

   Yet ere the burning wilderness be won,
Shines down on other deeds the shuddering sun.
City of Joseph[33]! Look! from 'leaguered walls,
Where Calvary's crimson light on Carthage falls! 2970

   Ere murderous fate the martyr's bolt hath sped,
While deepening darkness glooms a sky of lead,
And thundrous threatenings tone their notes of dread,
Looms to the fore an archangelic form,
A sunlit summit shining o'er the storm;
A towering rock above the rushing tide
Of eager souls that surge on every side,
Where living waters from the fountain play,
And glowing words light up the darkened way.

   Undaunted 'neath the shadow of his doom, 2980
Calm as a statue, solemn as a tomb,
Heedless of self, while hoarsely rumbles near
Hate's fiery flood, that alien to all fear,
That more than man, nor less than godlike soul,
Erect upon life's summit, at death's goal,
Unlocks time's portal, swings the future's gate,
And opes to Ephraim's gaze his glorious fate.

   O diver in the days and years to be!
Searching the caves of that prophetic sea,
What bringest from the deeps of destiny? 2990

CANTO TEN

The Parted Veil[1]

    Choice Seer, with spirit eye did he behold
The sanguine scene that told his tragic fate?
Surged by the flood of grief and shame that rolled
Above the murdered honor of a State[2],
Where innocence again fell prey to hate?
There be who say he visioned all to come—
Forsaken cities, weeping, desolate,
The desecrated fane, the blazing dome[3],
The weary wanderings far in quest of peace and home.

    Saw, then, a tender hopeful tragedy 3000
(Pathetic omen of his tribe's increase)
Uncurtained 'neath the star-hung canopy:
Babes, new-born babes[4], there slumbering in a fleece
Of moon-lit frost, as buds that bide release,
When winter casts its mantle white and cold,
Protecting life where life hath seemed to cease;
Frail lambs, fresh penned within the Saviour's fold,
And, like Him, manger-nurst, homeless on earth's threshold.

    Homeless a nursing nation, born e'en so—
Born in a day. O Day! and eyes of Night! 3010
Watch now the "little one" "a thousand"[5] grow,
As grows the torrent from the trickling height,
The blaze of noonday from the dawning light;—
The birth-throes of an empire, whose blest reign,
Bounding from lowliness, soars past the sight
Of all save prophecy, while cities twain[6]
Sceptre the universe, with foot on land and main!

    Whose but a prophet's eye such end could see?
Whose but a prophet's tongue the issue tell?—
A modern march of ancient destiny, 3020
Another Exodus and Israel,
Bidding his bonds, his all, save hope, farewell;
Widening, 'mid alien wastes, true freedom's fame,
Where bondage, chained to darkness, fain would dwell[7];
And rearing temples to Jehovah's name,
Where looms the Aztec's altar[8], quenched of its ancient flame.

There bringing forth the promise of thy land,
O rare and wondrous West!—the prophecy
Of glittering cities strewn along thy strand,
O golden empire[9] of the sunset sea! 3030
God-gifted Seer, while gazing endlessly,
Sawest thou an Eden on the desert brine[10],
Begirt with desolation's mystery,
Ere gusht the riven rock with milk and wine,
Where all was treeless waste and sun-baked alkaline?

Sawest thou, O prophet! till the pioneer
Builded his eagle nest, and pure and brave
Homed on the white-helmed peak and crystal mere?
O matchless land—the home their valor gave,
Mighty in will to bless, in work to save, 3040
Redeemed, redeeming, all must own thy worth!
Slander may wound thee, tyranny enslave,
Still thou art mine, loved land of all the earth,
Land of the honey-bee[11], land of my mortal birth!

Land prest by footprint of my pilgrim sire[12];
Land visioned by my more than sire, whose soul
Swept the far future with a glance of fire,
Bade hope, as memory, her page unroll;
Beheld uplifting, as a parted scroll,
The curtain from a kingdom yet to be, 3050
Binding in one world-realms from pole to pole;
Saw monarchs bow, saw nations bend the knee,
Saw dead and risen time take on eternity.

"Hear me, my people[13]! I shall not be slain
While unfulfilled my mission? Then, like Him
Who holds my hand, linked in an endless chain,
Which cannot die, whose light can ne'er grow dim,
Must I return to Home and Elohim.
Though here I fain would linger—human choice!
If weal to friend or foe—ay, e'en to them, 3060
Might purchased be, with my poor life the price,
Welcome, thrice welcome death. I will the sacrifice.

"Nor marvel at my mood. Could you but gaze
Upon the wonders of the worlds of God,
Where burn, amid the universal blaze,
The Father's fullness and the Son's abode,
Won by their feet who walk the rightful road,

Nor weary in well-doing; 'twere alone
Reward for all that here hath been your load.
Forgive—leave all to heaven, whose highest Throne 3070
Made endless love to endless life the stepping stone.

    "Hearken, O House of Joseph! Here must end
My mortal toil. Now, as from Nebo's height[14],
I see, like him of old, my day descend.
But looms afar upon my sinking sight
Another Canaan. Clothe for pilgrim flight.
A Joshua cometh! Him let Israel heed,
And loyal be unto that council's right
On whom the Kingdom rolls; for they must lead
To where privation's hand shall sow dominion's seed. 3080

    "A glacier's might, your gathered strength shall stand,
Stalwart upon the mountains[15], and shall send
Swift messengers to sound o'er sea and land
Last warning to the nations. Hither wend
Awakening hosts, who eager hearing lend
While yet the voice of grace, the voice of God,
Summons the house of Abraham his friend;
Calls them the wave to cleave, the wild to plod,
On, on to that safe rest, ere falls the reckoning rod.

    "For war shall wound[16] this nation—rend it wide, 3090
And trample nations all. Anon shall slaves
'Gainst masters rise, and anarchy o'erride
Till tyranny be trodden as the paves,
Till patriot might puts forth its hand and saves
The crimsoned land from chaos. Hearken, all!
When ruin's host the blood-red banner waves,
Who heeded first the Gospel's warning call
Shall be the last of realms to crumble and to fall.

    "Britannia! Thou among the during ones,
A nursing mother unto Israel's might; 4000
Foremost to send thy daughters and thy sons
From shores afar, from darkness unto light.
As thou hast favored truth and 'friended right,
Their tongues shall plead for thee in time to come,
And nerve thine arm when perilous thy plight.
Borne on thy shoulder o'er the billowing foam,
Joseph and Judah find their heritage, their home.

"I saw, while justice showed the vision dire,
Till mercy's hand let fall the lifted veil,
The goal of the ungodly—blood and fire, 4010
Earthquake and whirlwind, pestilential hail
Smiting earth's face with desolating flail.
And this, the mere beginning of their woe,
Whose final fate a doom the damned bewail;
While they that follow Christ, anon shall go
To guide and save lost souls, groping in shades below.

"Good fears not evil—grapples with it strong,
Hell turns to heaven, the unclean purifies;
For evil is but good, the right bent wrong.
No weakling unto loftiest worlds can rise; 4020
No coward e'er hath scaled celestial skies;
'Tis strength that wins the goal of blessedness,
'Tis knowledge saves, 'tis wisdom glorifies;
Intelligence alone can lift and bless
The fallen, innocent till snared in sin's duress.

"What matter, if my mortal race be run,
Where earth enfolds me to her mother breast?
While ye, my people—yonder setting sun
Points out your path. For you, no peace, no rest,
Till firm your weary feet upon the West, 4030
Where, moveless as yon snowy spine of hills,
Befriended by the tempest, unopprest,
And bounteous as the sun that sends the rills
To bless the vales, God's first-born fold[17] His purpose fills.

"Affliction here, but friendship there and peace;
(More cruel Christian white than savage red),
And in a day when warning tongues shall cease,
And plain be seen what prophets all have said;
When peace shall have no pillow for her head,
Save lofty heights where loyal hosts abound; 4040
Brave sons of battling sires[18], who toiled and bled
That this might evermore be freedom's ground,
Shall give to you their strength God's Kingdom here to found.

"Bide mountain-walled, my people! stalwart, strong,
Till poureth down from hallowed founts on high,
The might that doth to righteousness belong,
The might of faith, the power of purity—
Despair and terror to iniquity.

       Then, Ephra-Judah, who the hand shall bind
       That clears thy path before thee? Foes shall fly 4050
       As driven dust, as ashes in the wind;
 The crouching Lion springs, and He the prey shall find.

       "And by that power[19] shall Zion be redeemed,
       Yea, with a mighty hand, an out-stretched arm,
       With marvels, miracles, ne'er done nor dreamed
       Since wonder oped her eyes. The world's alarm
       Shall surge, an angry sea; but fear nor harm
       Can hover near the conquering host of God.
       'Gainst Lucifer's shall Michael's legions form,
       Besoming the chosen soil with chastening rod, 4060
 Till sainted towers arise on Eden's ancient sod.

       "The place appointed. Naught else is designed;
       Naught else can heaven accept. Put forth the hand,
       Plant stakes of Zion, tight her cords to bind,
       Where'er ye move, O fated pilgrim band!
       But bring forth Zion's self on Zion's land[20];
       The consecrated soil, whereon ye stood
       With me, of late, loyal while treason fanned
       The flame still thirsting for a martyr's blood.
 There build, in time to be, a city unto God. 4070

       "Nor there alone; for all is Zion's land,
       North unto South, East unto Western wave,
       Far as the hemisphere's wide wings expand,
       She sits, a sovereign queen, ice-crowned, to lave
       Her glowing hands in tropic tides, while brave
       Her snowy feet in faith the southern sea.
       Arm patient, slow to smite, yet swift to save,
       A friend to right, a foe to tyranny.
 And there be living now who then shall live and see.

       "While here the glory of the Common Good[21], 4080
       Shadowed and symboled by a patriot band,
       Whose triumph wrought for human brotherhood,
       Extending that high cause from strand to strand,
       Shall bring deliverance unto every land.
       But anarchy would foil the lofty aim,
       The peace, the union, by Jehovah planned;
       Wherefore 'tis doomed to failure and to shame,
 With all unrighteous rule, whate'er its place or name.

"The sceptered harlot,[22] throned on human seas,
  Chief link of Satan's world-encircling chain; 4090
The secret craft and crime—iniquities
  Whereby the Wicked One extends his reign;
All these must perish from the Lord's domain,
  Nor aught of guile be found His Kingdom through.
Truth's sun hath risen—all lesser lights must wane;
  And wrong and false that masks as right and true,
Shall feel the scourge of flame that Sodom's sin o'erthrew.

"More would I tell that in my bosom burns,
  But bigot fires would flame as ne'er before;
For truth, rejected, friend to traitor turns, 5000
  And damns where fain 'twould save. Six mounting o'er,
My spirit to a seventh realm[23] did soar,
  And saw and heard—Ah, would that I might say!
Though memory but renewed a former lore,
  What all may learn when full the dawning day,
When twinkling, twilight faith to knowledge shall give way.

"Hope not till then to have my history,
  What life hath scribed to scan; nor tongue nor pen
Can tell the tale, dispel the mystery,
  That hides me from the dim, dull gaze of men. 5010
Sojourning here, within this shadowed scene,
  A medial stage, a mortal compromise,
The spirit's might, the body's weight, between,
  Deem not that e'en earth's wisest can be wise,
Till heaven the blindness touch that seals all human eyes.

"One little fold I lift of that vast veil:
  How came he God, to whom all gods must bow—
The very Sire, whom all the sons now hail
  As mightiest of the mighty? I avow
That even He was once as we are now; 5020
  That we like Him can be—yea, by degrees,
Mount unto loftiest heights, till on each brow
  Be writ the Name of Names. Not angels these,
But Gods, e'en Sons of God, through all eternities.

"Weighed in the balance here, nor wanting found;
  Tried in the fire, triumphant from the test;
Though wrung their hearts, their finest feelings ground,
  Betwixt life's upper, nether, millstones prest,
Till proved, of good and brave, the bravest, best.

Less faith than theirs who follow Abraham, 5030
Honoring o'er all Jehovah's high behest,
Uplifts no gate of that Jerusalem—
The Bosom of the Gods—the Glory of I AM.[24]

   "Bide valiant here, as ye were valiant there.
Whence came delightsome bodies, soaring minds,
Aspiring thrones to win and crowns to wear?
Spring not all seeds according to their kinds?
Each act, each word, each thought, delivers, binds,
Dwarfs or develops. Man's all-crowning state
His own creation. What the Judgment finds, 5040
The soul reveals; and weal or woe the fate,
'Tis freedom's chainless choice, for all on will must wait.

   "Stand as ye stood, my legion brave, what time
The starry host, celestial symphony,
Choraled the anthem seraphic, sublime,
To the spelled ear of all eternity!
Lifted your hands for light and liberty[25],
When fraud with force progression's path would pave.
Fought we with Michael, drove the dragon, he
Who planned to seize all worlds, all worlds enslave, 5050
And would have damned, destroyed, what Christ came down to save.

   "As now, in lesser liberty's abode,
Incarnate spirit of fell tyranny
Would trample on the type of Freedom's Code[26],
Befriending human right where'er it be.
But hear me, Heaven! Come life, come death, to me,
Jehovah's captain, in His name and fear,
I vow to Him His people shall be free—
Ay, free all men, as in that former sphere, 5060
When hurled from yon dread height the power of Lucifer.

   "Fear not—Truth's cause shall triumph. Sown the seed
Whose harvest knows no failure, no delay.
Crooked shall straighten to the future need,
And crudeness unto culture shall give way;
And part shall change to perfect in that day.
Firm, strong—not smooth, the building's basic stone,
Hidden from view; while rests the heavenly ray
On polished wall, on gleaming spire and cone:
Jacob's, not Esau's hand[27] shall rear Messiah's throne. 5070

"Great the beginning—glorious the end;
Elijah comes, the Kingdom to complete[28].
Farewell! This from your father, brother, friend.
No more your prophet, patriarch, ye meet,
Till here all prophets, patriarchs, ye greet,
Mingling with Gods, while heaven on earth shall dwell,
To drink the wine of wisdom at His feet,
The Husbandman and Vine of Israel.
Thus saith the God of Jacob—Joseph's God. Farewell!"

—-

Then sank to rest, his mortal mission done. 5080
Hark to those shouts that hail a homing king!
A crimson aureole rounds the sinking sun,
Omen of golden dawn swift following;
Death's winter promise of eternal spring—
Celestial Edens, empires, throne on throne,
And worlds once waste, redeemed, there blossoming.
Future now present, and the past unflown,
While all unguised, unveiled, life, death, earth, time, are known.

EPILOGUE

The Angel Ascendant[1]

But what are life, death, earth, and time to thee,
Eternal Truth? Thou goest on for aye. 5090
Lives, deaths, earths, times, their plurals multifold,
These but the bubbles on thy boundless wave,
The sands of thy great glass, the flickering gleams
Of life that knows nor origin nor end.
These but the sparks flung from thy flaming forge,
The falling star-dust of thy firmament,
Where stars go down that straightway suns may rise.

Each ray of light, each principle of power,
Each epoch-measuring hap of history,
Had it a tongue would it not testify: 6000
"There cometh after me a mightier;
I but prepare the way his face before;
I but baptize with water, he with fire?"
Till now tells not the past this oft-told tale,
Which yet the future shall proclaim and prove?

Thou Angel, there ascending from the East,
Who criest unto four, Hurt not, but spare,
Till we the servants of our God have sealed!
Who art thou and why risest now to view?

"I am that Voice which crieth in the waste; 6010
That wandereth through all worlds, invisible;
That sayeth unto all, Prepare, prepare,
Behold He cometh! Go ye out to meet.

"As His, my goings forth are from of old:
A minister to Earth from Eden's hour,
Reopening the guarded heavenward way,
Whereby the fallen Michael rose again[2];
Lifting to rest the city sanctified[3],
Awaiting there my mandate to descend.

"Wrought I through him whom Gods name Gabriel, 6020
The Noah of a world once water-doomed,
By whom was earth besprent with life anew,
Nor less with light from truth's rekindled flame,
Still burning, though with error's incense dimmed,
And fouled with alien fire[4] in many lands.

"Wrought I through him whom men call Abraham,
The root of Shiloh[5], righteous branch of Shem;
Quarry of Israel, rock whence he was hewn;
Blesser of races with believing blood[6],
Sprinkler of spirits faithful o'er the world,   6030
Oceans of nations, fountainward that flow,
As the soiled floods unto the filtering sea.

"Led I when Israel cast Egypt's chain[7],
And cleft the wave 'twixt bonds and liberty;
As lead I shall when one the Shepherd loved
Bringeth the sheep from long captivity[8].
Smote I by him who carved to Canaan's land,
Whose sword[9] gave Israel his inheritance,
Whose high behest e'en day and night obeyed,
On Gibeon, in the vale of Ajalon.   6040
Blazed I through him who flamed as fire from heaven
At Kishon's brook[10], where sunk the pride of Baal;
Sealer, unsealer, of the sending skies,
Renewer of the worship primal, pure.
My hand in his, the anointed, named ere born[11],
To sunder brazen-gated Babylon,
Foreshadowing the great deliverance
Wrought out by Him who died all worlds to win.

"Then burst the long sealed canopy[12] o'er him
Revealed to whom were holy Sire and Son,   6050
And angel guardian of the book of gold;
That truth might vanquish error, and once more
Be known to men the true and living God.

"When spake the angels of authority,
Mine was the hand that gave the Kingdom's keys[13],
Lifting an ensign for the gathering;
Beginning of an ending yet to be,
When I a second time shall set my hand,
Judah, with Joseph, joining to the fold,
And long lost tribes and remnants ransoming.   6060

"The martyred Seer who gave up life to give
The warning unto Ephraim, God's first born,
Came I to him the Abrahamic keys[14],
The Abrahamic covenant, to restore;
That Jacob, to the end increasing still,
Might be as sands and stars for multitude.

"How tell the sum[15] of all my ministries?
Wrought I through him who gave to East the West,
Through him whose pen of fire proclaimed it free,
Through him whose blade the blood-bought soil redeemed. 6070
Came I to thee, lone muser on the mount,
My minstrel—I thy muse. Dost know me now?

"All, all that make for freedom and for peace,
That loose the captive, and the lost restore,
That teach, in part or whole, eternal truth,
By science, art, or might of melody;—
All these my ministers, who aid my aims.
Elias I, their tasks Elias-given.

"Spirit of Progress, speeding on for aye;
Gleam of the glory of Omnipotence; 6080
Hand of the Arm Omnific—cause of all;
A mighty making way for Mightier,
Coming, as Jacob upon Esau's heel[16],
Eternity upon the trail of time.

"Jehovah's ancient covenant Messenger,
Come I again, again, His courier,
Till plenal powers of great Melchizedek
The fullness of the glory here unfold,
Whelming, O Earth! as once with watery wave,
Thy form with fire, from founts of heavenly flame; 6090
Sealing, unsealing, binding o'er and o'er,
Till all is order, as of old ordained.

"Then shall the Watchman on the Wall proclaim:
'Be glad, O Zion and Jerusalem!
Rejoice, O Earth! No longer grieve and mourn.
Ended the empire of iniquity,
Broken oppression's rod forevermore.
Gone are the gold, the silver, and the bronze,
The conquering iron, and the crumbling clay;
World-wide, heaven-high, the Stone of Israel stands; 7000
The Chaldean image as the Chaldean dream[17]!'

"And who is She that looketh forth sublime,
Clothed with the sun, shod with the moon's pale beam,
Her matchless brow bediademed with stars?
Fairer than eve, mightier than bursting morn,
As noon-day majesty magnificent?

"Perfection, heaven-retained unto this hour,
Immanuel's Spouse, the glorious Bride of Christ,
Arrayed in all her garments beautiful,
Adorned and ready[18], waiting for her Lord! 7010

"Now, Heaven's loud trumpets, all Earth's secrets tell!
Death and hell's dungeons, liberate your dead!
For 'mid the shouts of saints, the risen, the changed,
Day dawns, hour strikes, skies burst—the King descends!

"Await that time destroyers four[19], who give
The Gospel, God's last warning unto man;
Await likewise the thousands, twelve times twelve[20],
Who for the coming King the way prepare.
Hold I the signet of the Living God—
Lift unto light, or hurl to darkness down. 7020
The hour is imminent. Heed well the sign:
Mark when the Bow's bright promise[21] is withdrawn!"

—-

Enough, I know thee, Strong and mighty One,
That standest in the presence of the Lord!
That leadest Israel from bondage old,
That liftest up the Ensign unto all!
Know thee, thou Muse and Minstrel of the Mount,
Thou Harper on the Hills of Melody?
I know thee, and am here to work thy will,
To hymn thy praise, perchance behold thy power, 7030
When, iris-crowned and clothed as with a cloud,
Thy face the sun, thy feet as pillared fire,
Thou comest down from Heaven, and swearest by
Eternity, that Time shall be no more!

Ancient of Ages! Angel of the East!
Spirit of Promise! Prophet of the Dawn[22]!

NOTES

Explanation: The first figure at the beginning of the Note indicates the word or phrase marked in the text; the second figure gives the number of the line in which it is found.

NOTE TO DEDICATION. The Dedication is to President Joseph F. Smith, sixth in succession to the leadership of the Latter-day Saints, nephew to Joseph the Prophet, and son of Hyrum the Patriarch, who were martyred at Carthage, Illinois, June 27, 1844. The poem made its appearance during President Smith's administration, and the author owes much to his kind encouragement and appreciation.

NOTE TO THEME. The words of the Theme are a passage from the "Key to John's Revelation" (Doctrine and Covenants 77:9).

NOTE TO PRELUDE. The Author, while ill, prayed that he might live to produce a work that would continue his ministry as a teacher after his mortal tongue was stilled. The beginning of the answer to his prayer was an immediate inspiration to write this poem.

—-

CANTO ONE

1—Title: **As From a Dream.** The subject of this Canto is the author's spiritual awakening.

2—20. **Baal and Astoreth** (also rendered Ashtoreth). Pagan deities, frequently mentioned in the Old Testament. They were worshiped by the idolatrous Israelites. The Prophet Elijah's controversy with the priests of Baal is one of the most dramatic episodes in sacred history. (I Kings 18:19-40). Baal was the sun god, chief male divinity of the Phoenicians; Ashtoreth, representing the moon, a goddess of the Philistines—the same as Astarte of the Zidonians. The corresponding deities among the Greeks and Romans were Zeus or Jupiter and Aphrodite or Venus.

3—60. **Truth's Triple Key.** The Spirit of Truth, revealing past, present and future.

4—86. **Ambrosial Gardens.** The Gardens of the Gods—Heaven.

5—92. **Paradise.** The Spirit World, a place of rest for the righteous, awaiting resurrection and exaltation to glorious spheres beyond. (Alma, 40:11-14; "Joseph Smith's Teachings," pp. 184, 185; Key to Theology, 14.)

6—101. **Love's Eyes.** Love is usually represented as a blind boy, Cupid, shooting his arrows aimlessly. Love, when spiritually enlightened, is no longer blind, but has a definite purpose in view.

7—111. **Lethean Ground.** Lethe, in classic mythology, signifies oblivion. It was the name of a river in Hades, of which the dead drank and forgot all.

8—117. **O Thou, Of Beauty!** The stanza beginning with these words is an apostrophe to Woman.

9—130. **Apple of Ashes.** On the shores of the Dead Sea there grows, it is said, a fruit resembling the apple, beautiful and inviting to the eye, but turning to ashes at the touch.

10—167. **Equally May Win.** The vanquished, as well as the victorious, may gain, through experience, development.

11—174. **What Soul Can Grow?** Pride, greed, hate, and all other perverted passions, are as weeds and thorns in the garden of the heart. It is fair to presume that the Saviour, when he exhorted his disciples to forgive and love their enemies, had in view the welfare of the disciples themselves. It was more for their sake than for the sake of their enemies, that He gave the exhortation.

12—185. **The Spirit of the Infinite.** The Holy Spirit, assumed throughout the poem to be acting through "Elias," the Genius of Progress, who also has his agents or instruments.

13—219. **Time's Hills and Vales.** A metaphor suggested by the Book of Abraham (3:18, 19).

—

CANTO TWO

1—Title: **The Soul of Song.** Herein the author is represented as soliloquising upon his native mountains, where he meets the Soul of Song and is inspired to sing the epic of time and eternity. As the Soul of Song, "Elias" makes his first appearance in the action of the poem.

2—261. **The Sacred Garden.** The Garden of Eden.

3—263. **Titan Stand.** The Titans were a group of mythical giants, descended from the gods. (Greek and Roman mythology.)

4—276. **Orphean Boon.** Orpheus, son of the Muse Calliope, received from Apollo or Minerva a lyre upon which he played so skillfully that rocks and trees were moved, rivers ceased to flow, and savage beasts forgot their wildness, charmed by the wonderful sounds. (Ibid.)

5—281. **Oh, Were My Words!** A paraphrase of Job 19:23, 24.

6—288. **Melting Gift.** The power of speech or of song.

7—384. **Voice of the Stars.** Another reference to Job (38:7).

8—390. **The Body's Bard.** This allusion is to poets who exalt the material over the spiritual, the sensuous over the intellectual, the body of things over the soul of things.

9—407. **This Most Ancient Shore.** Modern science, confirming modern revelation, is beginning to regard America as the Old World, not the New.

10—408. **And Man Shall Rise.** Zion, City of the Pure-in-Heart, is to stand upon the ancient site of the Garden of Eden.

11—415. **Shepherd Psalmist.** David, who played before King Saul, exorcising the evil spirit which held the monarch bound. (I Samuel 18:10 and 19:9.)

CANTO THREE

1—Title: **Elect of Elohim.** Elohim, or Eloheim, the Hebrew plural for God. To the modern Jew it means the plural of majesty, not of number; but to the Latter-day Saint it signifies both. As here used it stands for "The Council of the Gods," or, as in Psalms 82:1, "The Congregation of the Mighty." In that council or congregation was elected, before Earth was formed, the Redeemer of the World. (Pearl of Great Price—Moses 4:1-4; Abraham 3:22-28; Compendium p. 285.) This Canto glimpses the choosing of Messiah, the rebellion of Lucifer, the Saviour's descent to Earth, his crucifixion and return to Glory. It is the beginning of the poem proper.

2—450. **Olea's Silver Beam.** Olea, according to the Book of Abraham, is Moon; Shinehah (Shinea) Sun; and Kokaubeam, Stars. Kolob, according to the same authority, is a great governing planet "nigh unto the throne of God." (Abraham 3; D. and C. 76:25, 28.)

3—504. **Mighty Michael.** Michael the Archangel, leader of the hosts of Heaven against Lucifer and his rebellious legions, became Adam and fell from an immortal to a mortal state that he might become the progenitor of the human family.

4—516. **Tried Souls.** In "Mormon" theology "soul" means body and spirit combined, but in general literature, and especially poetry, "soul" and "spirit" are synonyms.

5—522. **The Stepping-Stone.** God's children, such as kept the first or spirit estate, were given bodies upon this planet, thus becoming souls, capable of eternal increase and advancement. (Abraham 3:26.) Two-thirds of the spirits then populating the Spirit World were found worthy of opportunities for experience and development in mortality, while one-third—those who rebelled—were denied that privilege. (Compendium p. 288.)

6—528. **The Love That Hath Redeemed All Worlds.** The Gospel of the Christ, the highest expression of God's love for man, has saved many worlds, and is destined to save many more. (Moses 1:33-39.) But the Gospel is more than a means of escape from impending ills; it existed before man had need of salvation. A divine plan for human progress, embracing both the Fall and the Redemption, it was framed in the heavens before this earth was organized, and is a free gift from God to man. Man, however, to avail himself of its benefits, must yield obedience to its requirements. Redemption (resurrection) comes unconditionally, but salvation and exaltation depend upon human works as well as upon divine favor. A soul may be redeemed—raised from the dead—and yet condemned at the final judgment for evil deeds done in the body. Likewise may a soul be redeemed and saved, and yet come short of the glory that constitutes exaltation. To redeem, save and glorify is the threefold purpose of the Gospel of Christ. The English word "Gospel" comes from the Anglo-Saxon "Godspell" or God-Story—the story of God. In its fullest sense it signifies everything connected with the redemptive career of that Divine Being who gave His life that man might eternally live.

7—548. **Exception Scorns.** Lucifer, who fain would have been the Redeemer, proposed to save by coercive methods, involving the destruction of human agency, and demanded as his reward the honor that belongs to God. (Moses 4:1-4; Abraham 3:22-28)

8—560. **My Messenger.** It was Jehovah the God of Israel who became Jesus of Nazareth and died to redeem mankind (D. and C. 110:1-4). He is Son Ahman, concerning whom Orson Pratt, citing an unpublished revelation, says: "What is the name of God in the pure language? The answer says 'Ahman.' What is the name of the Son of God? Answer, 'Son Ahman, the greatest of all the parts of God, excepting Ahman.' What is the name of men? 'Son Ahman,' is the answer." (Journal of Discourses, Vol. II, p. 342.)

9—562. **Thy Face Before.** An allusion to Elias, the lesser going before the greater.

10—571. **My Friend.** Abraham, the friend of God, and father of the faithful.

11—572. **Idumea.** The World—here used as a synonym for Earth.

12—589. **This Wandering Planet Bring.** "This earth will be rolled back into the presence of God and crowned with celestial glory."—Joseph Smith (Compendium, p. 288).

13—613. **The Hour of Noon.** The Meridian Dispensation.

14—615. **Light's Sun and Moon.** Christ, the light of the sun, moon and stars, and the power by which they were made. (D. and C. 88:7, 8, 9.)

15—619. **Elias? Yea and Nay.** John the Baptist, forerunner of the Christ, was an Elias, a restorer; but, according to Joseph Smith, not the Elias who is to restore all things. There are many Eliases, Joseph says: "When God sends a man into the world to prepare for a greater work, holding the keys of the power of Elias, it was called the doctrine of Elias even from the early ages of the world." (Compendium, p. 281.)

16—621. **Learned to Shine.** Before the Twelve Apostles were chosen, John the Baptist proclaimed the Lamb of God, and said concerning Him: "He must increase, and I must decrease." John was therefore as the waning Moon in the presence of the rising Sun.

17—640. **A City Doomed.** Jerusalem, over which the Saviour wept, prophesying its downfall. (Matthew 23:37-39.)

18—656. **Gloom-Wrapt Gethsemane.** The Saviour's agony in the Garden of Gethsemane is an incident familiar to every reader of the New Testament.

19—675. **Immanuel.** One of the titles of the Saviour, meaning "God with us."

CANTO FOUR

1—Title: **Night and the Wilderness.** This part of the poem is an allegory of the Christian or Meridian Dispensation, following the death of Jesus and his forerunner; portraying the mission of the Comforter, and showing the departure from the primitive Faith, after the passing of the apostolic Twelve, one of whom—the Church having gone into the Wilderness—remains to testify of things to come. The "Night" is the spiritual night that followed the setting of the Sun of Righteousness—a night lit by Moon and Stars, with lesser lights twinkling through the Dark Ages and onward into modern times. The "Wilderness" is the world invisible. (D. and C. 88:66.)

2—688. **An Eagle's Wings.** The Roman Empire, emblemized by the Eagle, dominated the then known world.

3—696. **Peace to Flow.** "(I) The immense field covered by the conquests of Alexander gave to the civilized world a unity of language, without which it would have been, humanly speaking, impossible for the earliest preachers to have made known the good tidings in every land which they traversed. (II) The rise of the Roman Empire created a political unity which reflected in every direction the doctrines of the new faith. (III) The dispersion of the Jews prepared vast multitudes of Greeks and Romans for the unity of a pure morality and a monotheistic faith. The Gospel emanated from the capital of Judea; it was preached in the tongue of Athens; it was diffused through the empire of Rome; the feet of its earliest missionaries traversed the solid structure of undeviating roads by which the Roman legionaries—'those massive hammers of the whole earth'—had made straight in the desert a highway for our God. Semite and Aryan had been unconscious instruments in the hands of God for the spread of a religion which, in its first beginnings, both alike detested and despised. The letters of Hebrew and Greek and Latin inscribed above the cross were the prophetic and unconscious testimony of three of the world's noblest languages to the undying claims of Him who suffered to obliterate the animosities of the nations which spoke them, and to unite them all together in the one great Family of God."—Dean Farrar, in "The Life and Work of St. Paul," abridged edition, Book II, pp. 61, 62.

4—706. **She-Wolf's Might.** The She-Wolf, traditionally the nurse of Romulus and Remus, who founded Rome, was also an emblem of that world-conquering power, which, though eventually it persecuted the Christians, at first protected them from their Jewish oppressors. Judah's emblem was the Lion. As for the remaining figure in the allusion, it is written that the Saviour said to his disciples: "I send you forth as lambs among wolves."

5—707. **Iron-Limbed.** The phrases "iron-limbed," "brazen-loin," "silver-breasted," "golden Babylon," characterize respectively the Roman, Graeco-Macedonian, Medo-Persian, and Babylonian empires, which, in reverse order, ruled successively the ancient world. Beginning with Babylon, the "head of gold," these four universal powers figure in the Prophet Daniel's interpretation of Nebuchadnezzar's dream (Daniel 2).

6—713. **Asian Kin.** Alexander the Great extended his conquests as far eastward as India, whose native inhabitants claim kinship with European peoples through a common Aryan ancestry. If this claim be true, then the Hindoos, like the Europeans, are descended from Japheth, the eldest son of Noah, and consequently are "Gentiles"—a word springing from "Gentilis," meaning "of a nation," that is, a nation not of Israel.

7—718. **Kurush.** Cyrus, founder of the Medo-Persian empire.

8—730. **Lofty Vineyards.** D. and C. 88:51-61.

9—731. **Spirit Moon and Speaking Stars.** The Holy Ghost and the Apostolic Twelve.

10—732. **The Woman Wonderful.** The Church of Christ, represented by a Woman (Revelation 12), and referred to in other places as the Bride, the Lamb's Wife.

11—736. **Glory's Symboling.** Sun, moon and stars, symbolizing celestial, terrestrial, and telestial glories. (D. and C. 76:96-98.)

12—742. **Vicegerent.** The Comforter, concerning whom Jesus said, "It is needful that I go, or He will not come unto you." In other words, the greater Light had to depart, before the lesser could shine in its fulness.

13—743. **The Unembodied One.** Says Joseph the Seer: "The Father has a body of flesh and bones, as tangible as man's; the Son also; but the Holy Ghost is a personage of spirit." (D. and C. 130:22.)

14—748. **After and Ere.** God and Christ, the Father and the Son, by the power of the Holy Ghost created all things, and by that power will raise all from the dead.

15—756. **Prophet Still Pleading.** The Spirit of Prophecy, typified by John the Baptist, preaching in the wilderness.

16—774. **Those Fluent Stars.** The Twelve Apostles, oracles of God and crown of the Church of Christ. (Rev. 12:1.)

17—781. **Save Haply One.** John the Beloved. (John 21:20-23; D. and C. 7 and 77.)

18—789. **Leading the Lost.** It is believed that John the Revelator will lead the Lost Tribes from "The Land of the North." (D. and C. 77:14; Rev. 10:8-11.)

19—806. **The Man-Child.** The Man-Child of the Apocalypse (Rev. 12:5) represents the Priesthood—divine authority—which was taken from the Earth, with the fulness of the Gospel, after the passing of the Apostles.

20—815. **Japheth Sways.** Gentile domination over Israel, particularly in those nations where the Jews have been and are still oppressed.

21—820. **Antaeus-Like.** Antaeus was a fabled giant, vanquished by Hercules. Each time that Hercules threw him the giant gained fresh strength from coming in contact with the ground.

22—822. **Conquering His Dust-Adoring Conqueror.** The modern Jew is said to hold the purse-strings of the world.

23—831. **That Gentile Hosts Might See.** Saul of Tarsus, afterwards Paul the Apostle, persecuted the Church of Christ before his conversion (Acts 9:1-19). Thus was typified the spiritual blindness of Israel, which caused the Gospel to be carried to the Gentiles. Paul, the principal agent for their illumination, declares: "Blindness in part is happened to Israel, until the fulness of the Gentiles be come in." (Rom. 11:25.)

24—832. **Martyred, Immolate.** Israel's dispersion, like Adam's fall and Christ's crucifixion, was part of a mighty plan for the promotion of the human race. Adam fell that mortal man might be. Christ died to burst the bands of death and make the fall effectual unto the higher ends ordained. The children of Israel were scattered over the world, in order that the Gospel might make its way more readily among all peoples. The history of Israel is the history of a martyred nation, suffering for the welfare of other nations, whatever may be said of the transgressions of the chosen people, which occasioned and justified the calamities that came upon them.

25—841. **From 'Neath the Yoke.** The future redemption of the Negro race.

26—843. **See and Hear His Risen Lord.** The House of Israel is privileged to receive the personal ministrations of the Saviour, while the Gentiles are ministered to by the Holy Ghost. (III Nephi 15:23.)

27—847. **In the Mire.** Beginning of the Christian departure from the true Faith.

28—850. **The Heaven-Lit Torch.** The Light of the Gospel, enjoyed by the primitive Christians, though compelled to hide from their Roman persecutors and worship God on mountain tops and in the catacombs.

29—852. **Incense * * * Diana's Shrine.** Diana was a deity worshiped by the Romans. "Incense"—metaphorically the vain philosophies, traditions and customs, adopted by the false Church that came up in the place of the true Church and paganized itself in order to be popular with the world.

30—855. **Shearing Compromise.** The result, spiritually, of the enthronement of Christianity as the state religion of the Roman Empire, A. D. 324.

31—861. **East from West.** The pseudo Church, as well as the Empire of the Caesars, divided itself into East and West, with Constantinople and Rome as the capital cities.

32—874. **She Was Wont.** "She" stands for the true Church of Christ.

33—880. **Crimson Courtesan.** The Scarlet Woman described by John the Revelator (Rev. 17).

34—900. **Till the Judgment Sits.** A reference to Daniel 7:21-27.

35—902. **Glory Lift the Gloom.** Messiah's second coming.

36—903. **The Moonlike One.** The Holy Spirit, ruling the Night of Ages, after the Light of the World has departed.

37—908. **Impelling to All Action.** The impelling power of the Spirit of God is interestingly set forth in I Nephi 13:10-19. See also Lowell's poems "Columbus" and "A Glance Behind the Curtain."

38—951. **Wayward Son of Deity.** Napoleon and other conquerors type the class of characters here described.

39—973. **Some Said Jeremias.** When the Saviour inquired, "Whom do men say that I am?" Peter answered "Some say Thou art Elias, and some say Jeremias." Elias and Jeremias are Greek forms of the Hebrew names Elijah and Jeremiah. Joseph Smith, however, drew a distinction between the spirit of Elias and the spirit of Elijah. (Compendium, pp. 281-283.)

40—983. **Mirror and Model of Humanity.** "God created man in his own image." (Gen. 1:27.)

41—997. **Incomprehensible.** So modern Christians contend respecting Deity. It is true only in part. God's unrevealed infinite fulness is of course incomprehensible to the finite mind. But what He has revealed concerning Himself is not incomprehensible. Else why did He reveal it?

42—1008. **Each as a Star.** The Jewish or Mosaic Dispensation shed light that prepared the world for a greater—the Christian Dispensation; which, in its turn, made ready for one greater still—the Dispensation of the Fulness of Times. This is the significance of "Elias." (Compendium, p. 281.)

43—1020. **A Weapon for the Right.** Such writers as Voltaire, Paine, and Ingersoll, subserve the cause of Christ by shattering false traditions, erroneously supposed by many to be true teachings of the Saviour and his Apostles.

CANTO FIVE

1—Title: **The Messenger of Morn.** The fore part of this Canto, down to and including the line, "Out, out of her, my people, saith your God," summarizes the message borne by the modern Prophet. The curtain now rises upon the last act of the redemptive drama—the final restoration of the Gospel; Joseph the Seer, as the Elias of the scene, heralding the tidings of the approaching millennial reign.

2—1052. **Whence Ye Were Hewn.** An allusion to Isaiah 51:1-3.

3—1060. **Wastes of Unbelief.** Gentile or heathen lands, refreshed by the sprinkled blood of Israel—the blood that believes—and by spiritual visitations that accompany or follow such dispersions.

4—1061. **Japheth, Thy Planet Pales.** Japheth stands for the Gentiles, whose "fulness" now "comes in."

5—1077. **Mother of Centuries.** Time, as distinguished from Eternity (though technically eternity includes time), comprises seven thousand years, or seventy centuries, covered by seven Gospel dispensations. The Quorum of the Seventy, with the presiding First Council, is a probable typing in this connection.

6—1079. **Teach Them to Be One.** "It is necessary, in the ushering in of the dispensation of the fulness of times, * * * that a whole and complete and perfect union and welding together of dispensations and keys and powers and glories should take place and be revealed from the days of Adam even to the present time."—Joseph Smith, (D. and C. 128:18.)

7—1084. **Shiloh Reigns.** Shiloh is another Hebrew name for Messiah, whose reign of a thousand years will equal in duration one revolution of the planet Kolob. (Abraham 3:4.)

8—1085. **Hast Labored.** The seven thousand years of Earth's "temporal existence" correspond to the seven seals of the Apocalyptic Book (Rev. 5 and 6) and are as seven great days, four of which had passed before Christ came, while nearly two have gone by since. According to this reckoning we are now in the Saturday evening of human history. The Millennium will be the seventh day—the World's Sabbath. (D. and C. 77:12; Abraham 3, 4, and 5).

9—1089. **Ancient Tidings.** The Everlasting Gospel, first revealed to Adam, who presides over all the dispensations. (History of the Church, Vol. 4, pp. 207-209).

10—1103. **What I Know.** Joseph Smith is said to have expressed the wish that he might reveal his identity and declare all that God had made known to him.

11—1117. **Gibborim.** Mighty ones. King David's six hundred guards were called "The Gibborim," for their heroic bravery. (Geike, "Hours With the Bible," Vol. III, pp. 254, 276, 325, 339).

12—1118. **Worthy The Word.** The explanation of this phrase is in that saying of the Saviour's: "Is it not written that they are gods to whom the word of God comes?"—meaning, of course, a superior race of men.

13—1136. **Fifth of Seven.** The Fifth Angel is he who "committeth the everlasting gospel." (D. and C., 88:103).

14—1165. **From Wintry Sleep.** At this point begins the personal history of the Prophet, who is also the subject of previous allusions. ("Writings of Joseph Smith"—Pearl of Great Price).

15—1214. **Dual Presence.** Joseph's vision of the Father and the Son.

16—1217. **Unknown Mount.** A mountain referred to in the Book of Moses. (1:1).

17—1235. **An Atlas.** Atlas was one of the Titans. He is depicted with the globe on his back.

18—1247. **Exalted Man.** "God himself is an exalted man."—Joseph Smith, ("Times and Seasons," August 15, 1844).

> "As man now is, God once was;
> As God now is, man may be."—
> Lorenzo Snow, Biography, p. 46.

19—1261. **Wisdom of the Wise.** The stanza in which this phrase occurs is based upon Isaiah 29:13, 14.

20—1283. **A Messenger From God.** The Angel Moroni.

21—1302. **Page to Page.** The Book of Mormon, or Stick of Joseph, joins with the Hebrew Bible, or Stick of Judah, as foretold by Ezekiel (37:16-20).

22—1310. **Ready For The Fall.** Prophecy ripe for fulfillment.

23—1311. **Elias Comes.** Moroni, restoring the Gospel, predicts the coming of a greater, to restore all things.

24—1324. **Fullest Freedom.** The Kingdom of God will protect all men in the enjoyment of their rights. The citizens and lawmakers of that Kingdom will not be all of one religious faith. So taught Joseph Smith and Brigham Young.

25—1331. **Primal Language.** The Adamic tongue or Pure Language, brought back in the restoration of all things.

26—1407. **Ramah * * * Cumorah.** Book of Mormon names. That book is an abridged history of two great races, the Jaredites and the Nephites, who inhabited America prior to its discovery by Europeans. Their occupancy of the land was successive, the Jaredites coming from the Tower of Babel, B. C. 2218; and the founders of the Nephite nation from Judea, B. C. 600. The Jaredites perished about the time that the Nephites came. The latter were destroyed, A. D. 384, by the Lamanites, a degenerate and savage faction of their own people, whose remnants were found by Columbus and named Indians. The golden plates containing the Nephite-Jaredite record were taken by Joseph Smith from the Jaredite hill Ramah, called by the Nephites, Cumorah.

CANTO SIX

1—Title: **From Out The Dust.** A paraphrase of Isaiah 29:4. The prediction is held to have been fulfilled in the coming forth of the Book of Mormon. This entire Canto is based upon the general content of that volume. It embodies the prehistoric story of America, assumed to have been related by the angel custodian to the translator of the buried Book of Gold.

2—1415. **Must Righteous Be.** See Ether 2:8-12.

3—1434. **Former State.** The Book of Mormon is the only adequate explanation of the origin of the American Indians.

4—1457. **Ancient Altar.** Adam's altar, in Adam-ondi-Ahman, otherwise Spring Hill, Daviess County, Missouri, (D. and C. 116; History of the Church, Vol. 3, p. 388).

5—1461. **Dual Grave.** Burial in earth and hell, or death temporal and spiritual.

6—1466. **Where Adam Dwelt.** According to Joseph Smith, Jackson County, Missouri, is the ancient site of the Garden of Eden. Our First Parents, after their expulsion from Eden, dwelt in the Valley of Adam-ondi-Ahman. See Note 4.

7—1468. **Still Chaste.** The fall of Adam and Eve, while technically a sin because of a broken law, should be stressed as the means whereby God's children obtained their bodies, rather than as an act of moral turpitude. There are two general classes of crimes—malum per se and malum prohibitum. Malum per se is a Latin phrase signifying "an evil in itself," while malum prohibitum means "that which is wrong because forbidden by law." The transgression of our First Parents was malum prohibitum, and the consequent descent from an immortal to a mortal condition was the Fall.

8—1470. **Love's Work.** Adam's fall prepared the way for Christ's redemptive mission. Had there been no fall, man would have remained a spirit, without a body, and consequently imperfect. Christ redeemed the soul—spirit and body—and put it in the way to perfection.

9—1471. **Zion of Primeval Days.** The City of Enoch. (Moses 7:18-64; History of the Church, Vol. 4, pp. 209, 210; D. and C. 84:99-102.)

10—1479. **Final Change.** The change wrought upon the people of Enoch by translation not being equivalent to resurrection, they will have to undergo a further change, to prepare them for celestial glory. But they will not taste of death. A similar lot is that of John the Beloved (John 21:20-23; D. and C. 7); also of the Three Nephites (III Nephi 28) and of certain ones mentioned by Paul (I Cor. 15:50-54).

11—1480. **New Jerusalem.** The divinely chosen site for the Holy City is Independence, Jackson County, Missouri.

12—1484. **Japheth * * * Shem.** The reference is to Noah's blessing upon Shem and Japheth (Gen. 9:26-27). From Shem came Abraham, the ancestor of the House of Israel; and from Japheth the Gentiles, the founders of the most enlightened nations of modern times, including the United States of America. Ham, through Canaan, was the progenitor of the negro race, long held in slavery in this and other Gentile countries. The Ethiopian has also served the Semite, as Noah predicted. How Japheth has "dwelt in the tents of Shem," is partly shown by the history of Palestine, long dominated by the Gentiles, particularly the Turks, who still possess it. Japheth's remarkable blessing has also been realized in the history of our own country, America, which the Gentiles now inhabit, and where, according to the Book of Mormon, they are to assist in gathering Israel and building the New Jerusalem, (III Nephi 20 and 21). It is their privilege to share, if they will, in all the blessings promised to the chosen people. (Abraham 2:9-11.) "The tents of Shem" may be interpreted to mean the homes of the people of God, lineally descended from Shem, through Abraham.

13—1485. **An Ark of Peace.** "It shall be the only people that shall not be at war one with another." (D. and C. 45:69).

14—1486. **The Ensign.** The Church of Christ in Latter Days.

15—1487. **Joseph Signals Jacob.** Joseph, in Ephraim, begins the work of Israel's gathering.

16—1489. **Ancient of Days.** Adam as the Ancient of Days will return to the place where he blessed his posterity. (D. and C. 116; History of the Church, Vol. 3, p. 388). See notes 4 and 6.

17—1507. **Hesperia.** The West—America.

18—1512. **That Servant.** The servant mentioned by the Saviour to the Nephites. (III Nephi 21:10, 11).

19—1515. **God's Legion.** "Zion, which shall come forth out of all the creations which I have made." (Moses 7:64).

20—1517. **Land of Joseph.** America, as the Latter-day Saints have been taught to believe, was given to Joseph of old as an inheritance. (Gen. 49:22, 26; Deut. 33:13-17).

21—1519. **Gog and Magog.** Gog is the name of a person; Magog, of a country or people. According to Ezekiel (38 and 39) Gog, "the chief prince of Meshech and Tubal," was to come with his people from the North to invade the land of Israel and there suffer defeat. Gog and Magog are generally understood as symbolical expressions for the heathen nations of Asia, more particularly the Scythians. In this poem the allusion is to those nations that war against Zion.

22—1538. **Where, Joseph?** Joseph Smith is meant. To him, after a general introduction, Moroni relates the story of the Jaredites, as told in that part of the Book of Mormon entitled "The Book of Ether."

23—1540. **Wide Severing.** In the days of Peleg the earth was "divided" (Gen. 10:25). Whether this means the dividing "to the nations" of "their inheritance" (Deut. 32.8), or a tearing asunder of the land into continents and islands, is not stated. The latter view, the one here suggested, may help to explain why the site of the Garden of Eden is now in North America.

24—1543. **Sons of Shinar.** The Jaredites, who came from the Tower of Babel, the place of which was "a plain in the Land of Shinar." (Gen. 11:2). Shinar was Chaldea.

25—1547. **Primal Tongue.** The language of the Jaredites—the pure Adamic tongue—was not confounded.

26—1554. **A Book Sublime.** A book written by the Jaredite leader, and yet to come forth. That leader was Mahonri Moriancumr, though this name does not occur in the Book of Mormon. "The Brother of Jared" is the only appellation bestowed upon him there. Joseph Smith supplied the missing name.

27—1557. **Baptismal Billows.** The Jaredites, in barges, passed through the depths of the ocean, to reach their Land of Promise (Ether 6:6). Their voyage was therefore a baptism, more literal than the passage of the Israelites through the Red Sea, and referred to by Paul as a baptism. (1 Cor. 10:2.)

28—1561. **Shelem's Height.** The Mount Shelem, so called "because of its exceeding height." (Ether 3:1).

29—1566. **Wing-Like Continents.** North and South America.

30—1573. **Mahonri's Realm.** North America, possessed by the Jaredites down to about 600 B. C., when the nation was destroyed by internecine strife.

31—1580. **Freedom's Greater Cause.** The Cause of Christ.

32—1591. **Past Zions Rose.** "Thou hast taken Zion to thine own bosom, from all thy creations, from all eternity to all eternity." (Moses 7:31.)

33—1595. **Fortressed by God's Mightiness.** I Nephi 13:19; Ether 2:12; D. and C. 45:70.

34—1601. **"Give Us a King."** The Jaredites demanded a king—a demand reluctantly acceded to by their leaders, who foresaw, as did Samuel the Prophet, in a similar situation, the evils that would result. (Ether 6:22-28; I Samuel 8:4-22).

35—1645. **Solitary Twain.** The Prophet Ether and King Coriantumr, the last of the Jaredites.

36—1653. **Another Nation.** The Nephites.

37—1657. **After Tale.** These words—part of a brief comment by the author—introduce a summary of the Nephite narrative.

38—1665. **A Leper.** Jerusalem in her degenerate state.

39—1666. **Prophet Pioneer.** Lehi, a descendant of Joseph, through Manasseh, with a colony from Jerusalem, succeeds the all but extinct Jaredites upon the Land of Promise, where they extend the glory of their great ancestor.

40—1669. **Joseph's Bough.** "Joseph is a fruitful bough." (Gen. 49:22).

41—1690. **Chosen Seer.** Lehi predicts the coming of "a choice seer" who is to be a lineal descendant of Joseph. The name of that seer is also to be Joseph, and it is to be the name of his father—a prophecy fulfilled in Joseph Smith, Jr. (II Nephi 3.)

42—1692. **Buried Lore.** The Book of Mormon.

43—1695. **Favored Son.** Nephi, who succeeded his father Lehi, and against whom his brothers Laman and Lemuel rebelled, thus dividing the nation into Nephites and Lamanites.

44—1712. **Heavy Rod.** The Lord used the savage Lamanites to scourge the enlightened yet ofttimes disobedient Nephites.

45—1717. **Infinite and Spirit Minister.** The Spirit of the Lord, declared by Nephi to be in the form of man, and with whom he conversed as one man converses with another. (I Nephi 11:11).

46—1731. **Prophet Prince Foresaw.** Nephi's vision of the future, in which he beheld events upon both hemispheres—Christ's crucifixion and resurrection, and his subsequent appearings to the more righteous of the Nephites, preceded by awful judgments upon the wicked (III Nephi 8-11).

47—1757. **Final Doom.** The conflagrations that destroyed Nephite cities were prophetic of the end of the world, which is to be by fire.

48—1771. **Infant Innocence.** The children of the Nephites, blessed by the Saviour. (III Nephi 17:11-24).

49—1785. **Other Sheep.** Jesus said to his Jewish disciples, "Other sheep I have, which are not of this fold." (John 10:16). They supposed that he meant the Gentiles, instead of which, as the Book of Mormon tells, he had reference to the Nephites and to other branches of the House of Israel. (III Nephi 15:17-24; 16:1; 17:4.)

50—1803. **Japheth's Destiny.** The Saviour portrays the future of America and the diverse fates of the obedient and disobedient Gentiles (III Nephi 16 and 21).

51—1811. **A Lion to the Chase.** III Nephi, 20:16; 21:12.

52—1820. **Sun's Red Glow.** The wrath of the Lamanites, turning upon their white oppressors.

53—1822. **Eternal Rays.** Divinely revealed laws by which Zion will be redeemed (D. and C. 105:4, 5).

54—1826. **Servant Marred.** "He shall be marred because of them." (III Nephi 21:10.)

55—1834. **He Sanctifieth Three.** The Three Nephites (III Nephi 28).

56—1847. **Forebeam of Day Divine.** The happy condition of the Nephites, for two centuries after the coming of Christ, was a foretaste of the Millennium.

57—1854. **So Shall It Be.** Terrible calamities are to precede the Reign of Peace, as they preceded the events that typified it. (Matthew 24).

58—1869. **Avalanche * * * Sun's Face.** Nephites and Lamanites.

59—1872. **Bloody Chase.** The Lamanites driving the Nephites to their doom at the Hill Cumorah.

60—1883. **Oriental Sight.** The Western Hemisphere discovered by the Eastern.

61—1885. **Faith * * * Patience.** The Brother of Jared was noted for his exceeding faith (Ether 3:9). Columbus triumphed by patient endurance.

62—1894. **Zion's Land.** Joseph Smith declared the whole of America to be the Land of Zion.

63—1899. **Oppressed Become Oppressors.** Even the liberty-loving settlers of New England, who had fled from tyranny in the Old World to find freedom in the New, enslaved the red man and drove him from his ancient possessions.

64—1904. **The Motherland.** Great Britain, mother of the New England colonies.

65—1909. **Man of Matchless Worth.** Washington.

66—1922. **Joseph's Namesake Seer.** Joseph Smith, Jr., (II Nephi 3).

67—1931. **The Iron Rod.** The Word of God (1 Nephi 11:25).

68—1945. **Spirit Gardens.** The Heavenly fields. (D. and C. 88:51-61).

CANTO SEVEN

1—Title: **The Arcana of the Infinite.** "Arcana," the Latin plural of "Arcanum," signifies hidden, secret. This title is intended to be an equivalent for "The Mysteries of the Kingdom"—the esoteric features or advanced principles of the Gospel. Herein are summarized those sublime doctrines that came directly to the modern Revelator during and subsequent to the translating of the ancient plates. A vision of the dispensations is involved—the reading of the Book of Time and the Volume of Eternity.

2—1986. **One Vast Mind.** Joseph Smith, Prophet, Seer, and Revelator.

3—2009. **The Solemn Dispensations.** In theology the term "dispensation"—from "dispense," to deal out or distribute—signifies the method or scheme by which God has at different times developed his purposes and revealed himself to man. It also denotes a period marked by some particular development of the Lord's work, such as the Mosaic Dispensation, lasting from Moses to Christ; or the Meridian Dispensation, ending in the apostasy that made necessary another restoration of the Gospel and the Priesthood. While revelation is silent upon the subject, it is probable that there are seven Gospel dispensations—seven distinct periods during which the Plan of Progression, revealed from Heaven to Earth, has been among the children of men. The belief as to seven is partly based upon the scriptural or symbolical character of that number, and upon the Prophet Joseph's teachings relative to the seven periods, each of a thousand years, answering to the seven seals of the mystical Book seen by John in his vision on Patmos (Rev. 5, 6; D. and C. 77).

4—2022. **The Trumpets Seven.** The Angels of the Dispensations. (D. and C. 88:92-116).

5—2032. **The Holy Order.** The Eternal Priesthood—divine authority—and those who wield it, in Heaven and on Earth. (History of the Church, Vol. III, p. 385; Vol. IV, p. 207; D. and C. 20, 68, 84, 107, 112, 121, 124; Alma 13:1-10.)

6—2057. **Ere Earth Knew Abraham.** The pre-existence of the House of Israel is intimated by Moses (Deut. 32:7, 8). The 144,000 mentioned by John (Rev. 14:1) and by Joseph (D. and C. 77:11) were "of all the tribes of the children of Israel."

7—2059. **Ark of God * * * Sword of Flame.** Emblems, respectively, of the Priesthood and the Gospel.

8—2063. **Shine and Shadow.** Dispensations of heavenly light, alternating with periods of spiritual darkness.

9—2068. **Succeeded By The Less.** Moses, with the Melchisedek Priesthood and the fulness of the Gospel, was taken back to Heaven, leaving Israel to be governed by the Aaronic Priesthood and the Law. (D. and C. 84:19-28.)

10—2071. **Ministers Upon Each Hemisphere.** Jewish and Nephite apostles.

11—2074. **The Perfect Church.** The Church of Christ on Earth, perfected after the pattern of the Church in Heaven. (D. and C. 76:67; 107:93. See also "Gospel Themes," p. 81.)

12—2089. **The Ancient One.** "Daniel, in his seventh chapter, speaks of the Ancient of Days; he means the oldest man, our father Adam, Michael; he will call his children together and hold a council with them to prepare them for the coming of the Son of Man."—Joseph Smith (History of the Church, Vol. 3, p. 386; D. and C. 116).

13—2099. **Keys of Light.** "Three grand keys by which good or bad angels or spirits may be known." (D. and C. 129).

14—2136. **Most Intelligent.** "God himself, finding he was in the midst of spirits and glory, because he was more intelligent, saw proper to institute laws whereby the rest could have a privilege to advance like himself."—Joseph Smith ("Times and Seasons," August 15. 1844).

15—2140. **Intelligence Eternal.** "Intelligence, or the light of truth, was not created or made, neither indeed can be" (D. and C. 93:29, 36). "The first principles of man are self existent with God." ("Times and Seasons," August 15, 1844).

16—2150. **Birth and Death Are Baptism.** See "Gospel Themes," pp. 66, 67.

17—2161. **Earthly Sorrow.** The trials of mortal life, foreseen from spirit heights by the children of God, who nevertheless rejoiced at the prospect of glory beyond.

18—2167. **Second Estate.** Man's first estate is the spirit life; his second estate, the mortal life. In the former he walks by sight, in the latter by faith.

19—2188. **Sun or Moon or Varying Star.** The heavenly bodies typify celestial, terrestrial, and telestial glories. (D. and C. 76:96-98.)

20—2197. **Vicarious Ordinance.** Temple work, done by the living in behalf of the dead. (D. and C. 127 and 128.)

21—2288. **Felon's Debt.** "This earth was organized or formed out of other planets which were broken up and remodeled and made into the one on which we live."—Joseph Smith (Compendium, p. 287).

22—2293. **Law Hath Magnified.** "The earth abideth the law of a celestial kingdom." (D. and C. 88:25).

23—2298. **Celestial Seer Stone.** Earth in its sanctified, immortal, and eternal state will be like a sea of glass and fire (Rev. 4:6), a great Urim and Thummim to its glorified inhabitants (D. and C. 130:6-11).

24—2325. **Would Have Lived The Law.** Men's desires as well as deeds will form a basis for eternal judgment (History of the Church, Vol. 2, p. 380).

25—2333. **Judah's One and Joseph's Three.** John the Revelator and the Three Nephites.

26—2336. **Unclothed Spirit.** The Spirit seen by the Brother of Jared, and afterwards embodied as Jesus of Nazareth.

27—2337. **The Triple Seer.** The Apostle Paul, "caught up to the third heaven" (II Cor. 12:2).

CANTO EIGHT

1—Title: **The Lifted Ensign.** The Church of Jesus Christ of Latter-day Saints, organized April 6, 1830.

2—2357. **Shepherds Twain.** Joseph Smith and Oliver Cowdery, the first and second Elders of the Church.

3—2366. **Giant of Untruth.** The parallel begun in the first stanza continues through the second.

4—2380. **Time Yet Was Young.** Here the main narrative reverts to the story of Enoch and his city, as revealed to Joseph the Seer, and embodied in the Book of Moses (6 and 7). In the poem that story continues as far as the line, "And Noah's righteous seed in me rejoice."

5—2389. **Sainted Commonweal.** The City of Enoch.

6—2400. **Chain * * * Sundered.** The people of Enoch, under the Law of Consecration, attained to such a superior condition that it was said of them: "And the Lord called his people Zion, because they were of one heart and one mind and dwelt in righteousness, and there was no poor among them." (Moses 7:18.)

7—2404. **Armageddon's Conflict.** The final struggle between the powers of Good and Evil, when Satan will be overthrown (D. and C. 88:112-115).

8—2409. **Terrestrial Radiance.** "Their place of habitation is that of the terrestrial order." They are "held in reserve to be ministering angels unto many planets," and "as yet have not entered into so great a fulness as those who are resurrected from the dead." Joseph Smith ("History of the Church," Vol. 4, pp. 209, 210).

9—2420. **The Captive Free.** Christ, during the interval between his crucifixion and resurrection, visited and preached to "the spirits in prison"—spirits disobedient in the days of Noah, and swept away by the Deluge (I Peter 3:19, 20; and 4:61; Key to Theology 14).

10—2424. **Climbing Robber-like.** According to the Bible, the people who built the Tower of Babel did so that its top might "reach unto heaven" (Gen. 11:4). Joseph Smith is said to have declared that the "heaven" they had in view was the City of Enoch, then suspended within sight of the earth. Endeavoring to get to Heaven by "another way," the builders of Babel were comparable to "thieves and robbers." Tradition asserts that the City of Enoch stood where the Gulf of Mexico now is.

11—2432. **Tri-Branching Tree.** Noah and his three sons, Japheth, Shem and Ham.

12—2464. **One Like Unto Him.** Joseph Smith was a man like unto Moses, who was like unto Christ. Moses led Israel out of temporal bondage, and Joseph began a work destined to deliver Israel from spiritual bondage. Thus Moses and Joseph were both typical of Him who redeemed the world from the bondage of sin and death.

13—2467. **A Two-Fold Type.** The social and spiritual condition of the Jewish saints and the Nephite disciples foretokened the Millennium. Joseph Smith had in view the realization of what Enoch had achieved, and what the primitive Christians endeavored to accomplish, in preparing a people for the presence of the Lord.

14—2473. **Sought Fulfillment.** Following these words is a description of social conditions at the time of the advent of "Mormonism."

15—2604. **The Trampled Terror.** A personification of the French Revolution.

16—2607. **Frowning Mass, Contemning Class.** The social problem of the Twentieth Century.

17—2630. **Time An Enoch Came.** Joseph Smith is likened unto Enoch, and even called by that name, in some of the early revelations (D. and C., 78, 92, 96, and 104). This may have been done to impress the fact that Joseph's work was similar to that of Enoch.

18—2656. **A Holy Hand.** John the Baptist, ordaining Joseph and Oliver to the Aaronic Priesthood, May 15, 1829 (D. and C. 13).

19—2661. **Panoply of Power.** The Priesthood. The main narrative here resumes from the point of digression.

20—2694. **Again The Woman Wonderful.** The Church of Christ in its Latter-day Restoration.

CANTO NINE

1—Title: **Upon the Shoulders of the Philistine.** Under this caption, suggested by Isaiah 11:14, is treated the westward movement of the Latter-day Saints, incidental to the gathering of scattered Israel.

2—2722. **Eaglet's Nest Is Empty.** Within a year after its organization the church migrated from its birthplace, Fayette, Seneca County, New York, and the surrounding region.

3—2724. **Storied Strand.** The shore of Lake Erie, in Northern Ohio, where the Saints began to settle early in 1831. There they built their first Temple, and took initial steps toward founding the United Order, under the Law of Consecration.

4—2742. **Shinea's Land.** Kirtland, Ohio, and its environs, was "The Land of Shinehah" (D. and C. 82:12 and 104:40-48). From that part, in 1837-38, the Church moved its headquarters to Far West, Caldwell County, Missouri.

5—2750. **Their Powers Bestow.** An allusion to visions seen in the Kirtland Temple, April 3, 1836 (D. and C. 110).

6—2759. **Laman's Bands.** The first mission to the Lamanites (Indians) was undertaken in the autumn of 1830. The missionaries labored also among the white people of Ohio and Missouri. At Independence, which was then on the frontier of the United States, they crossed the line into Indian Territory, now the State of Kansas.

7—2767. **Lands the Rarest.** The region drained by the Mississippi and Missouri rivers.

8—2779. **Japheth's Wrath.** The Gentiles in Western Missouri, misapprehending the motives of the "Mormons" in gathering to that part, and incited by evil-minded agitators, rose against the newcomers, and drove them first from Jackson County, and eventually from the State.

9—2788. **The Shoulders.** Civilization, with its steamships, railroads, and other utilities, and persecution, with faggot and sword, have helped God's people to accomplish their destiny. "The blood of the martyrs" has been "the seed of the Church," whose every movement, voluntary or compulsory, has been toward the goal of its ultimate triumph.

10—2791. **Calm Caesar.** Julius Caesar, while crossing a stormswept water, quieted the apprehensions of his boatman by remarking, "Fear not, you carry Caesar and his fortunes."

11—2794. **The Law of Liberty.** The Gospel of Christ, misnamed "Mormonism."

12—2800. **Sees Menace.** Having come mostly from the North and the East, the "Mormons" were suspected by the slave-holding Missourians of being abolitionists. This false charge, with others equally groundless, caused the persecution that followed.

13—2813. **A Second Pharaoh * * * A Herod.** These epithets fitly characterize the Governor of Missouri, Lilburn W. Boggs, who issued the edict under which the persecuted people were expelled. Said he, to the mob-militia who drove them from their homes: "The Mormons must be exterminated or driven from the State."

14—2815. **Gathering the Whirlwind.** Missouri paid her debt to justice during the Civil War, when her Western borders, where mob violence had assailed her "Mormon" citizens, were ravaged again and again by the fierce guerilla warfare that spent its fury in that unhappy region.

15—2829. **Shakes the Dungeon.** Joseph Smith and others were imprisoned in Richmond Jail, where they were taunted by their guards, who boasted of murders and outrages committed upon the defenseless people after the surrender of Far West. The lion-hearted leader endured it till he could endure no more. Springing to his feet, he rebuked the ribald wretches, commanding them in the name of Jesus Christ to be still. They obeyed, cowering before him and begging his pardon. Parley P. Pratt, a fellow prisoner with the Prophet, says of this remarkable incident: "He ceased to speak. He stood erect in terrible majesty, chained and without a weapon. * * * I have seen the ministers of justice, clothed in magisterial robes, and criminals arraigned before them, while life was suspended on a breath in the courts of England; I have witnessed a Congress in solemn session to give laws to nations * * * but dignity and majesty have I seen but once, as it stood in chains at midnight in a dungeon, in an obscure village of Missouri." (Autobiography, pp. 229, 230.)

16—2835. **Disease and Death Subdued.** After the Prophet had regained his freedom, and while his followers were settling at Commerce (afterwards Nauvoo), an epidemic of fever and ague swept over that region. Many, prostrated by the malady, were miraculously healed under his administrations.

17—2836. **Sire of Waters.** The Mississippi River.

18—2839. **City, Mother of Many.** Nauvoo the Beautiful, built upon the site of Commerce, in Hancock County, Illinois, was the parent and model of many other cities subsequently founded by the Latter-day Saints, mostly in the region of the Rocky Mountains.

19—2846. **Unworldly Link.** The Nauvoo Temple, where work began in this dispensation for the salvation of the dead.

20—2847. **Elijah's Mightier Mission.** Malachi 3:1 and 4:5, 6; D. and C. 110:4-16; History of the Church, Vol. 4, p. 211; Gospel Themes, pp. 138, 139.

21—2860. **Crisis Past.** Early in 1837, during a period of apostacy at Kirtland, the Prophet said: "Something new must be done to save the Church." Thereupon he appointed Heber C. Kimball, of the Council of the Twelve, to head a mission to Europe. Part of the opposition encountered by Elder Kimball and his associates was a fierce onslaught by evil spirits, at Preston, England, where they began their labors. (Life of Heber C. Kimball, pp. 138-146.) The first company of emigrating Saints from abroad sailed from Liverpool for Nauvoo, in 1840. By that time another apostolic mission, headed by Brigham Young, President of the Twelve, had been sent to the British Isles.

22—2863. **Befriended by the Just.** Many of the people of Illinois extended a hospitable welcome to the plundered and homeless "Mormons," fleeing out of Missouri.

23—2866. **Earliest Offering.** Ephraim is the first branch of the Israelitish tree to bear the fruits of faith in and obedience to the Gospel in latter days. "Ephraim is my first-born," the Lord says through Jeremiah (31:9). That is, Ephraim, who "mixed himself among the people" (Hosea 7:8), is the first to be "born of God"—baptized and gathered out from the nations.

24—2877. **Egypt of the West.** America, where the gathered descendants of Joseph are to re-enact upon a larger scale the part played by their great ancestor in the famine-stricken nation on the Nile.

25—2882. **Long Lost Captives.** The Ten Tribes, carried away by the Assyrians, B. C. 721, and who are to return from "the north countries" (D. and C. 133:26-35).

26—2891. **Rallying the Loyal.** The Latter-day Saints have been taught to look forward to a time when they, lifting up an ensign to lovers of law, order, and liberty, and reinforced by them, will save this Nation, while anarchy is aiming at its life.

27—2903. **Inglorious Battleground.** The field of Cumorah.

28—2905. **Where Erst He Fled.** The House of Joseph, in modern times, begins its march of destiny at the Hill Cumorah, where the Nephites (also of Joseph) met their tragic fate. There is a tradition to the effect that every Temple reared by the Latter-day Saints marks a stage in the flight of the doomed Nephites, pursued by the victorious Lamanites, to the final slaughter at that historic hill.

29—2919. **Ruined Lie.** The allusion is to cities and temples built and abandoned by the Saints in Ohio, Missouri, and Illinois. (D. and C. 101, 103, and 105.)

30—2924. **Union * * * Enoch Saw.** The United Order—all things consecrated to God. (D. and C. 105:4, 5.)

31—2930. **Her Trembling Foes.** "Let us not go up to battle against Zion, for the inhabitants of Zion are terrible." (D. and C. 45:70.)

32—2951. **Pain Shall Bring Thee Power.** Sacrificial trials, that purify and elevate, redound to the advantage of posterity. The parents suffer that the children may be blest. All noble and powerful races have "come up through great tribulation."

33—2969. **City of Joseph.** A name given to Nauvoo after the Prophet's martyrdom.

—

CANTO TEN

1—Title: **The Parted Veil.** Joseph's vision and prophecy of the future. He is represented as foretelling to his people their great destiny.

2—2994. **Honor of a State.** Joseph the Prophet and Hyrum the Patriarch were murdered while under the pledged protection of the Governor of Illinois. The mob that fired its fatal volleys into the bosoms of the martyrs, and went unwhipped of justice, struck down the honor of a sovereign commonwealth of the American Union.

3—2998. **The Blazing Dome.** The Nauvoo Temple, burned by the mob forces, after they had captured the city and expelled the remnant of the persecuted community left behind at the beginning of the exodus in February, 1846.

4—3003. **New Born Babes.** Nine infants, it is said, were born in the camps of the fugitive Saints, on Sugar Creek, Iowa, the first night out from Nauvoo.

5—3011. **Born in a Day. "Little One"—"A Thousand."**—Applications of ancient prophecy. (Isaiah 60:22 and 66:8).

6—3016. **Cities Twain.** Zion and Jerusalem, the future capitals of the Saviour's Kingdom; the former the seat of representative government, the latter of monarchical power. "Out of Zion shall go forth the law, and the word of the Lord from Jerusalem." (Isaiah 2:3; Micah 4:2.)

7—3024. **Fain Would Dwell.** The extension of slavery to the West was the dream of the South before the Civil War. This was one reason why the Southern States favored the war with Mexico.

8—3026. **Aztec's Altar.** The region settled by the "Mormon" people, between the Rocky Mountains and the Sierra Nevada, belonged to Mexico, the Land of the Aztecs.

9—3030. **Golden Empire!** California, as a Mexican province, included the present States of Utah and Nevada. Some of the earliest settlers of Salt Lake Valley had previously helped to colonize California, and were among those who discovered gold there, January, 1848.

10—3032. **Eden on the Desert Brine.** The redeemed Wilderness surrounding the Great Salt Lake, and formerly known as "The Great American Desert."

11—3044. **Land of the Honey Bee.** The State of Utah.

12—3045. **Pilgrim Sire.** The author's father, Horace Kimball Whitney, was one of the Pioneers who entered Salt Lake Valley, July 24, 1847.

13—3054. **Hear Me, My People!** At this point begins the Prophet's farewell address. The preceding stanzas of this Canto are a generalization of what follows in detail.

14—3073. **Nebo's Height.** Joseph, compared to Moses, is predicting his own death and the coming of his successor, the President of the Twelve, upon whom the Prophet placed the right of succession.

15—3082. **Stalwart Upon the Mountains.** At Montrose, Iowa, August 6, 1842, Joseph Smith predicted that the Saints would be driven westward, and would "become a mighty people in the midst of the Rocky Mountains."

16—3090. **War Shall Wound.** On Christmas Day, 1832, the Prophet foretold the war between the North and South. (D. and C. 87.) According to tradition, he also declared that those nations that first received the Gospel in this dispensation, would be preserved when "the consumption decreed" "made a full end of all nations."

17—4034. **First Born Fold.** Ephraim, fulfilling his mission in the region of the Rocky Mountains.

18—4041. **Brave Sons of Battling Sires.** Descendants of the patriots of the American Revolution.

19—4053. **And by that Power.** "The redemption of Zion must needs come by power." (D. and C. 103:15.)

20—4066. **Zion's Land.** Zion in a restricted sense—Jackson County.

21—4080. **The Common Good.** Christ's Commonwealth, foreshadowed by the American Union.

22—4089. **The Sceptered Harlot.** The Woman described in the Apocalypse as sitting "upon many waters"—a "great city" reigning "over the kings of the earth." (Rev. 17.)

23—5002. **A Seventh Realm.** Joseph, paraphrasing Paul, said concerning himself: "I know a man who was caught up to the seventh heaven."

24—5033. **I Am.** The Name Divine. (Ex. 3:14.)

25—5047. **Light and Liberty.** "At the first organization in Heaven we were all present and saw the Saviour chosen and appointed, and the plan of salvation made, and we sanctioned it."—Joseph Smith (Compendium, p. 288).

26—5055. **Freedom's Code.** The Gospel of Christ, "the perfect law of liberty," typed by the American Constitution, guaranteeing freedom and equal rights.

27—5070. **Not Esau's Hand.** Culture as well as strength must play its part in the building up of God's Kingdom. Zion, at first primitive and crude, shall become "the perfection of beauty," "the joy of the whole earth." Her original builders may be likened to the massive, immovable foundations of a structure whose polished walls and glittering spires are represented by their children, educated under improved conditions, and yet to stand in the forefront of the world's civilization.

28—5072. **The Kingdom to Complete.** "The spirit and power of Elijah is to come after, holding the keys of power, building the temple to the capstone, placing the seals of the Melchisedek Priesthood upon the House of Israel, and making all things ready; then Messiah comes to his Temple."—Joseph Smith (Compendium, p. 283; D. and C. 27).

EPILOGUE

1—Title: **The Angel Ascendant.** The Angel ascending from the East (Rev. 7:2; D. and C. 77:9). This is Elias, an address to and a response from whom forms the body of the epilogue, or final division of the poem.

2—6017. **Rose Again.** Elias the All-restorer is represented as reopening for Adam the closed communication between Earth and Heaven.

3—6018. **The City Sanctified.** The City of Enoch.

4—6025. **Alien Fire.** The Gospel, restored through Noah, standing at the head of a dispensation, was carried by his descendants, after the Flood, to various parts of the earth, where fragments of it remain, mixed with the traditions of men. Ceremonies similar to, or suggestive of Gospel ordinances, and found among primitive peoples, are thus accounted for.

5—6027. **The Root of Shiloh.** Abraham, ancestor to Jesus of Nazareth.

6—6029. **Believing Blood.** "How, by the dispersion of the children of Abraham, was the promise to the patriarch fulfilled, that in him and in his seed should all the nations of the earth be blessed? * * * By this dispersion the blood of Abraham, Isaac, and Jacob—the blood of faith, the blood that believes—with choice spirits answering to that blood, and selected for that purpose, were sent into those nations where the Gospel was afterwards preached, spirits capable of recognizing the truth, and brave enough to embrace it." (Gospel Themes, p. 156.)

7—6033. **Egypt's Chain.** The spirit of Elias was upon Moses when he led Israel out of bondage.

8—6036. **Long Captivity.** The Assyrian Captivity, which carried away the ten tribes.

9—6038. **Whose Sword.** The sword of Joshua, the conqueror of Canaan.

10—6042. **Kishon's Brook.** It was at the Brook Kishon that Elijah slew the Priests of Baal.

11—6045. **Named Ere Born.** Cyrus, the conqueror of Babylon, who restored the captive Jews, was named by Isaiah more than a century before his birth. (Isaiah, 45:1.)

12—6049. **Long Sealed Canopy.** The Heavens at the opening of the Last Dispensation.

13—6055. **The Kingdom's Keys.** The Melchisedek Priesthood. Elijah "holds the keys of the authority to administer in all the ordinances of the Priesthood." (History of the Church, Vol. 4, p. 211; D. and C. 2.)

14—6063. **Abrahamic Keys.** Elias, in the Kirtland Temple, "committed the keys of the Gospel of Abraham." (D. and C. 110:12.)

15—6067. **How Tell the Sum?** This stanza associates Columbus, Jefferson and Washington, impersonally, with others previously mentioned, as agents of Elias.

16—6083. **Jacob Upon Esau's Heel.** Genesis, 25:26.

17—7001. **Chaldean Dream.** The nations represented by the image seen in Nebuchadnezzar's dream, are to pass, like the dream itself, which the king was unable to recall.

18—7010. **Adorned and Ready.** When the Church, the Bride, is fully prepared, the Lord, the Bridegroom, will come.

19—7015. **Destroyers Four.** Four angels (Rev. 7:1; D. and C. 77:8, 9).

20—7017. **Twelve Times Twelve.** The One Hundred and Forty-Four Thousand. (Rev. 14:1; D. and C. 77:11.)

21—7022. **The Bow's Bright Promise.** Joseph the Seer gave, as a sign of the Second Coming, the withdrawal of the rainbow. Christ would not come during any year that the rainbow was visible; but when it was permanently withdrawn, the world might know that His coming was near at hand. (Compendium, p. 83.)

22—7036. **Prophet of the Dawn.** Elias, the Morning Star.

End of the Project Gutenberg EBook of Elias, by Orson F. Whitney

Ingram Content Group UK Ltd.
Milton Keynes UK
UKHW040654100723
424847UK00004B/514